4/14

IDENTITY THEFT

DO'S & DONT'S
WHAT YOU NEED TO KNOW

WHAT YOU NEED TO DO
NOW WHAT?

(Based on Actual Events)

Written by:

Scott A. Merritt

& ASSOCIATES INC.

"Planning with Merit"

P.O. Box 725
Bay City, MI 48707
517-292-2105

www.planningwithmerit.com

Library of Congress Control Number: 2013923413
ISBN 978-0-9910449-0-0

Table of Contents

Foreword

This book was written to help others not to go through what I experienced and continue to deal with. It is in no way to be deemed legal advice but merely an account of what I endured, continue to go through and what to do and what not to do along the way. This book is written based on actual events in story format and actions to be taken along with key hints during the journey to reclaiming one's identity. During this journey you will be challenged emotionally, financially, in terms of character, one's reputation and will face many degrees of frustration and stress throughout the process. This book is intended to lead one through the path of identity recapture and minimize the anguish during the daunting process.

As outlined by my firm's mission, vision, values and priorities, the goal of this book is to serve as merely a single step in one's long-term success personally, professionally and financially. I wrote it to further this initiative far beyond those of my personal clients and to hold others in the industry to a higher standard and aid the public in the process of selecting competent financial advisors. This book's focus is on the foundation of one's financial success, his or hers credit worthiness and reputation. This is an asset that all people start with on their balance sheet but not all are able to retain it. Some lose it due to their own actions while others lose this valuable asset as a result of others' actions. This book has been prepared for the layman as the first step in the process of recapturing one's identity following an identity theft. This process will allow an individual to reinsert this critical building block back on to his or her personal balance sheet. For one to build success of any kind without such an asset present they are constructing their building on far more than a cracked foundation. It is being poorly built on quicksand and it is merely a matter of time before the weight of one's success will cause the whole structure to collapse. But those who invest the time and effort take this necessary step will build success that will last for many generations to come.

Mission, Vision, Values, Priority

Merritt & Associates Inc.

"Planning with Merit"

Vision

To develop a Team of Professional Financial Advisors offering a comprehensive variety of products and services established and maintained through integrity based, trustworthy, and enduring relationships.

Mission

To provide a systematic and complete process with state-of-the-art resources that will meet all the financial needs of our clients. Our team will be comprised of experts in every area necessary to assist our clients in reaching their desired financial endeavors.

Values

We place honesty and integrity above all, always respecting the spiritual choice of everyone. Our focus is to work with each client always putting forth measures that ensure the protection of our client and our firm's best interest.

Priorities

We will support and defend the civil liberties within the borders of our country while enhancing and desiring everlasting relationship with our families, clients, and our team. Our behavior will always reflect the highest level of moral and ethical conduct.

Bio

Scott A. Merritt is the CEO and sole stockholder of Merritt
Ventures, Inc. DBA Merritt & Associates. Merritt & Associates,
Inc. is a wholly owned subsidiary of Merritt Ventures, Inc. Mr.
Merritt has more than a decade of experience in the real estate
industry, financial planning, insurance, investment services,
and has more than a decade in mortgage services. He also
recently organized a realty venture group that sold real estate
in various locations throughout Michigan at a level over three
million dollars. He is the head of the holding company, Merritt
Ventures, Inc. and its control group of subsidiaries and holds a
registered securities, security supervisory license. Mr. Merritt
also holds a life, accident and health insurance license, and
a principal associate real estate broker's license. He has an
Associate's in Pre-law, Bachelor's in Business Administration
and certificate in computer information systems from Ferris
State University. He has personally represented himself in
court more times than most attorneys have appeared in court.
He is not an attorney but has become an informed expert in
the areas of identity theft and credit correction. He grew up in
Michigan, in the Midwest region of the United States. He has
worked for numerous political officials as both a campaign aide
and congressional intern. This business and political experience
has exposed Scott to the inner workings of the government both
at the state and federal levels. This knowledge further aided him
in his self-taught use and enforcement of the laws relating to
identity theft and credit correction.

"HOUSE OF FINANCIAL SUCCESS"

Good Foundation

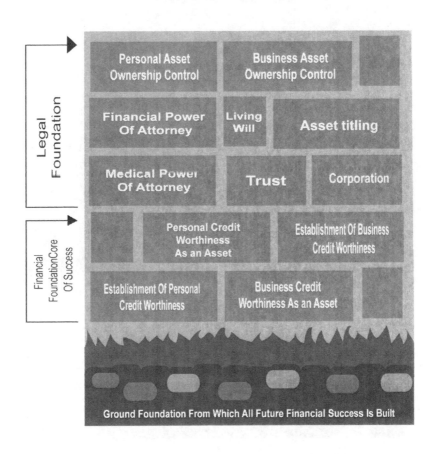

("FOUNDATION OF FINANCIAL SUCCESS" CHART)

House Of Financial Sucess

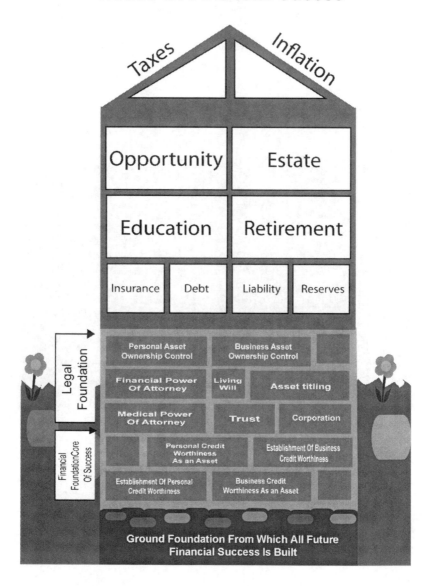

Chapter 1
The Calm Before the Identity Theft Storm

This story begins in early 2006. I was sitting in my Bay City, Michigan office on a sunny early spring afternoon opening my mail like any other day. I opened an envelope from one of my banking institutions. Inside was a letter informing me that one of the bank's processing centers had recently been broken into. This was chilling to me due to the number of accounts I had with this institution both personally and professionally for my businesses. I immediately opened all of my other banking envelopes within my pile of mail and scanned them very closely. In reviewing them I found no cause for concern. However, as a precautionary measure I stopped into a local branch of the bank and showed them the letter I'd received. They pulled up each account and we verified no improper activity. Little did I know this would dramatically change in the weeks ahead and the events to follow would change my life for many years to come if not forever.

I returned to my office initially confident but still somewhat skeptical that I had no reason for concern. I then received my next group of statements a few weeks later and I still saw no reason for concern.

In the coming months this would become the worst episode in my life and continues to haunt me to this day. In late March 2006 I once again received my statements but noticed several transactions that were not familiar to me. I inquired at a local branch and referenced the previously received letter that I had subsequently thrown out when I thought it was not relevant a few weeks earlier. This was the second worst decision I made in this matter and would prove problematic for me later on. However, even though I went to the same branch and spoke to the same person, she had no recollection of the conversation and they had no idea what I was talking about, as if the prior conversation never took place. The bank employee then told me that they never sent me a letter stating their processing center had been broken into. I found this conversation very disturbing knowing not only that I had received the letter but more importantly that the prior conversation had indeed taken place.

HINT:
Never throw anything away until at least a minimum of ten years has passed. If it's a report such as a police report, or directly related to identity theft, then retain it forever. No exceptions.

I promptly left the branch and went to another branch, and they said they had no knowledge of any processing center breach. I showed them the unknown transactions and after considerable conversation they did nothing. The dollar amounts were nominal and the bank would do nothing. In essence I was forced to pay for these fraudulent transactions and all fees resulting from them.

I was frustrated at this stage so I contacted my legal service I had on retainer at the time to get advice on how to proceed. They said the matter would be assigned to an attorney within three business days and that the assigned attorney would call me. The three days passed and the attorney called me and I outlined the situation and they told me to do the following:

TO DO LIST

- File a formal objection to the bank charges and fraudulent transactions with the bank
- File a police report claiming identity theft
- Secure a copy of my credit report from each of the credit reporting agencies individually (do not use a merged credit report)

HINT:
Be persistent but polite as when you attempt to file a police report many times your request will be denied

(1) The above to do list seems both logical and relatively simple. Let me advise you this will be one of the hardest parts of the process and one of the most frustrating. I went to the bank and procured the last six months printouts of all accounts and compared them to my statements and marked the erroneous transactions and associated fees on the printout. I then went to a local branch and attempted to file a complaint but they refused to comply with my request.

They did however agree to change all of my accounts, debit cards, PINs, etc. for each account. I thought this was a good approach. However, I would later learn that the initial request (closing the accounts and opening entirely new accounts) was both required to be complied with and the better of the options. As I later learned, what they did was essentially copy all of my old information over to a newly aligned debit card. This however did not stop the problem as it still indirectly tied it to the old account. This process in spite of the multiple requests was repeated on more than four occasions and each with the same result.

HINT:
Make sure they do not simply realign the account and reissue a new debit card and PIN. Rather, see to it that they issue a fully new account, debit card and PIN assigned to a new account number and that the old information is not realigned under the new account but that the old account is (marked) closed per your request.

(2) Filing the police report will be one of the most bizarre processes you will go through. I went to three police departments and they all refused to file the report and all actually accused me of being dishonest! This will mark the beginning of being treated like a criminal rather than the victim, so be prepared. However, you will need to be persistent in this regard and insist on speaking to a supervisor until your request is fulfilled. If you sense you will not get any assistance at the police station then you can either wait for another shift or you can try another precinct or station in your area. I found

the state police to be absolutely useless in the beginning but they will be useful once you have established that an identity theft has in fact occurred.

I also found the city police tend to dismiss the matter and do not even treat it as an investigative crime. I then tried the local sheriff's office and found them to be at least willing to take my complaint. I met the officer at the station and he took my complaint and filed a one-page police report. In this report he denoted that I was a victim of identity theft. Be prepared with copies of each credit bureau individually as well as any account statements that have fraudulent transactions present on them and proof that you have objected to the charges in writing either by a company complaint form or by a letter sent by certified mail. Lastly, if you are aware of how the theft occurred or the source of the identity theft, be sure to make this known.

HINT:

Make certain to get the police report number, officer's card and date when report will be available for copy to be retrieved. Once available procure a copy of the report and make several copies of it. Organization right from the start is key to long-term success in recapturing your identity.

These initial steps of filing an objection with your bank, securing a copy of each credit bureau report and a copy of the police report took nearly 90 days to complete. It is crucial for you to understand that the key to success early on in this process includes:

- being persistent
- being diplomatic but firm when dealing with officials
- only answering a question when asked and only answering those questions that are relevant to getting the requested item you need (many times they will try to trip you up to avoid fulfilling your request).

HINT:

You do not want to have to carry your social security card and other items with you regularly while fighting your identity theft. Place a copy of your driver's license and social security card on a single sheet of paper and make copies, as every time you make a formal request this will need to be attached. If you have an updated address on the back be sure to make the copy noted above and then recopy it with the backside also included on the single page and use this as the master copy.

* **Do not** use a color copy as this violates federal
law, i.e. the Patriot Act (black & white only).
If you ignore this and use color they will ignore
you altogether even if submitted in person.

Having filed a formal complaint with the bank, I thought that surely I would be remunerated for the false bank charges and unauthorized activity in my account. Wrong. As I noted earlier, after a long conversation I was forced to not only endure the fraudulent charges but pay the associated bank fees. If you give in and pay you have admitted responsibility so do not make the mistake I did and give in. I took this approach so as not to damage my relationship with the bank and to avoid the need for concern with regards to legitimate checks I had written.

HINT:

Regardless of what the institution says, they do not care about you no matter how long you have done business with them. I will cover this in greater detail later on. The bank's sole purpose is to minimize potential liability at all costs.

I then went to the main office to speak with a bank VP and surely I thought I would recoup my losses that by this stage in the game were beginning to mount considerably in terms of dollars due to the numerous fraudulent transactions and the related bank fees. The VP in one breath expressed empathy and in the other contempt at the mere fact that I would even suggest that they were involved in any way in such actions or lack of actions.

It was from this meeting that I began to realize I was the one being forced to provide the burden of proof. So I contacted my legal service once again and I ended up sending them copies of the documents I had relating to the fraudulent transactions up until that point. They reviewed the items and prepared a legal letter to the bank. This was met with far more contempt than you can possibly imagine. The bank's legal counsel responded immediately and they made numerous false allegations against me and in essence began to portray me as the fraudster instead of the victim. After numerous letters back and forth no ground was gained. Their sole tactic was to wear me down both emotionally and financially, figuring if they kept objecting I would eventually give up. I finally turned the matter over to the Consumer Protections Department. One would come to think that their objective is to protect the public from gross misconduct of this type. Let me be clear: this is not their objective at all in any way. This was a lesson I learned the very hard way.

While this varies in format, agency name, department names and similar items from state to state, each state has a series of consumer protection divisions covering a wide array of topics from banking, insurance, trades and professional services. While they are portrayed as consumer protection entities, they are truly in the pocket of the very institutions they oversee. You see, people formerly in the private sector and previously with large firms in these industries typically run these agencies. They contribute huge amounts of money to elected officials that oversee these agency managers in an effort to influence how the agency interprets and enforces the laws within its purview. In an effort to expose at least some of these perverse "protections" I will cite a few examples from my home state of Michigan. I have intentionally omitted the representative's names to avoid being accused of slander or defamation of character. Kind of ironic don't you think. I will however, at the end of this book in the reference section give you the sources to locate the enforcers of these laws in your own state.

Let me start by naming a few agencies and the industries per market segment that they oversee. I have focused this list on those that will later on claim to be your source of assistance in recapturing your identity and good name. It is important to also understand that these agencies and officials run both within the state realm as well as the federal realm. Many times, to avoid taking action one will try to pass the matter off to the other, hoping to place it in the crack as a non covered matter. This will happen far too many times to count.

HINT:
Determine if it is a state or federal matter specifically before contacting agency. How to do this will be explained in a later chapter.

A mere sampling of the alleged protectors:

OFIR:
Office of Insurance & Regulation: this organization oversees many regional banks (appointed by elected officials)

OCC:
Office of the Comptroller of Currency: oversees organizations involved in currency activities and national banks (appointed by elected officials)

FTC:
Federal Trade Commission: To be the primary cop of these agencies' enforcement (appointed by elected officials)

Public Service Commission:
This is an organization that oversees utilities and acts as a liaison when disputes arise with various public utilities. They have their own grievance process but it is highly skewed against the consumer and it is an ineffective organization.

Attorney General:
To serve as the lawyer for the state or federal government and

address matters that need to be dealt with such as misconduct of a regulated company (elected to position).

Governor:
To serve as the manager of all of the above (elected to position)

State Representative:
Elected to serve as consumer liaison when unable to get an agency or regulator to act properly.

State Senator:
Elected to serve as consumer liaison when unable to get an agency or regulator to act and state representative is unsuccessful or unwilling to aid in your request, which is very common.

U.S Congressman:
Elected to serve as consumer liaison when unable to get an agency or regulator to act with regards to a Federal agency. I have found this to be one of the most effective people you have at your disposal. These people are elected and they want to keep being elected and they have the resources in terms of staff and clout to make agencies work on matters effectively. While this will vary from area to area, some of these officials have actual liaisons within the very agencies in question that report to their office directly and only assist their constituents with such matters.

U.S. Senator:
Federal liaison used when the agencies, congressman and other resources have failed and either should not have or was unable to get the matter looked at, which is very common. However, again be sure to exhaust personal dispute actions, agency contacts, and other liaisons before going this route. The senator's office will want to know that you warrant assistance because others have failed to do so or have been ineffective at accomplishing the objective in question (elected to position, tends to handle tougher agency matters).

*_HINT:_

Be sure to do a series of disputes and inquire yourself before enlisting assistance as they are not your personal staff but are a resource to be used when you can not get an agency to do their job.

This is merely a sampling of agencies and agency governing officials at your disposal and many others could have been listed. This large bureaucracy is one of the problems that causes identity theft and its clean up to be so difficult. Again, recognizing if what you are dealing with is a state or federal matter will serve you greatly in determining which agency, which official and when to contact. This determining process will be outlined in greater detail in a later chapter.

Chapter 2
Beginning the Battle and Knowing It

Continuing on with my story, while one might think that what I've described so far covers a great deal of time, nothing could be further from the truth. In fact, at this stage we are a mere four months into what has become a five-year battle and is still going as of the writing of this book. However, I do want to give you hope as I am now roughly 75 percent of the way home and this was delayed due to many derailment that I have yet to outline but will as I outline the events. These events, some good and some bad, are meant to show you both what to do and what not do while working to recapture your identity and your reputation.

Up until this point I have focused the story on the bank where the identity theft occurred. However, you need to realize that there are many more facets to the situation than just the source bank. First there is the fact that I had both numerous personal accounts as well as business accounts with this source bank where the theft occurred. This caused the event of the theft to not only impact me personally and my personal credit but also to impact my businesses and business credit that also had accounts at the bank. This damaged the reputation of not only myself but my entities that were also impacted. It brought with it such things as multiple bank fees in these accounts, fraudulent charges much the same as noted earlier but on a larger scale, as these were business accounts. As a result the accounts were changed in the same fashion as noted earlier, having redirected the accounts with new PINs and cards, but not solving the problem even after multiple attempts.   Each time this occurred I had to call and notify all the hundred plus vendors that auto deposited or auto debited accounts. Many times I would not even get through the entire list before having to start all over. This got to a point of utter confusion for both myself and for the vendors involved. Moreover, it caused checks to bounce and have to be reissued. Credit lines had to be eliminated, and the companies put on a cash basis, further negatively impacting cash flow and company growth. This was all on top of the ongoing theft through the fraudsters and of course the bank that was being paid an absolute gluttony of fees unjustifiably. Each time I though it was solved it would start all over. Think of this as if it were a tumultuous heavyweight boxing match, sometimes giving solid blows other times receiving them.

By this point there had developed a hateful relationship with a number of the branch personnel who would intentionally look busy when I walked into the branch so they did not have to serve me or better yet take the person behind me and leave me standing there unserved. When this began to happen yet another event occurred that completely caused any previously gained ground to be lost.

What was this you ask? It was simple, but would be yet another event that would put me months behind. I had numerous business subsidiaries under my parent company and as a result I had these other subsidiary accounts at other institutions. The source bank that caused the theft then bought another bank I was doing business with. This became problematic on multiple fronts. First, it caused this other business subsidiary to become impacted negatively by the prior identity theft. I began having the same problems with this business' accounts as I was having with the prior outlined accounts. Money being taken and charges imposed and so on. However, it went far further than this as for one thing I could not legally have the two accounts at the same bank per contracts and operating agreements. This meant that I had to move one of the accounts, which once again involved considerable expense and time setting up another account, notifying all of the vendors that auto deposited of this company and auto debited. The irony here was I'd just gotten everything established at the firm that was just purchased by the source bank!

This caused many of the investors, partners and other related parties to develop concern as to why this was occurring and made me look bad. At one point, allegations were made that something shady was going on. In an effort to alleviate this concern I wrote a formal letter to all parties explaining the fact that the identity theft had occurred and that the source bank had purchased the other bank and that the two accounts could not be at the same institution per contracts. This put them at ease but they were still concerned that this event may impact the company in a negative fashion. I went to the prior mentioned source bank's VP and explained the position they'd put me in by buying the bank, and then stiffing me with the costs and time of relocating the account. They acknowledged that this was a direct result of their actions and returned costs to relocate the account to another institution, as it was apparent that their purchase had resulted in the need for the change.

This went smoothly and I got the new account set up and investors, partners, clients and others calmed down. However, it was like the calm before the storm as up to this point we have primarily talked about the source bank where the identity theft occurred and the bank accounts I had to move. But there were much larger impacts to be considered.

You see, once the thieves got my information from the bank processing center they had huge amounts of information about me, my companies, account balances, where I had other accounts, account sizes, typical transaction sizes and on and on. This caused an influx of fraud and theft from accounts like you have never seen. Again remember each time these thefts occurred I had to not only cover the thefts, but the bank and vendor charges that resulted. It simply got to a point where I could no longer keep up nor could I get the floodgates shut off fast enough. Several of my business accounts were hit very hard. This caused further hardship as not only did I have to cover the losses, and explain it all to my partners and investors, it began to impact these divisions' ability to do business and grow. This began to not only impact me financially but my partners and investors as well. It made for some very ugly conversations to say the least, and got to a point where I was trying to cover thousands weekly and it was simply not sustainable long-term unless something changed.

One of the partners thought, why don't we eliminate all of the other partners, he would put up the money and I would continue to run things as my actions were sound but the identity theft was the problem. So we took this approach and all seemed well. Do keep in mind we are now at the end of summer of 2006, less than six months have passed since the identity theft first occurred. I had purchased my home sometime earlier on a land contract and long before the identity theft and it was now time to refinance it. Given the identity theft I knew this was going to be tough even though I had completely renovated the home, bought under market and had a fair amount of equity in it. The lender said I had to pay off all of the derogatory items. I once again consulted with the legal group on retainer and explained the situation. The firm had been disputing the fraudulent accounts one by one but given the volume I had been dealing with noted above I was making very little progress on the individual matters as I primarily was busy trying to work, putting out the fires noted earlier up until that point.

I asked them if I pay these off, would it negate my ability to be reimbursed later? They said that for the most part it should not, on most matters. But given my situation I should go ahead and do so, but to make sure that each creditor that was part of the fraud to be listed on the HUD-1 separately. That way it could be shown how they were paid in full from the equity in my home later on when the time came to do so.

HINT:
DO NOT make this mistake. Refuse to pay anything resulting from fraud.

I proceeded to get my loan ready for mortgage and was able to do it through my mortgage relationship at the time but received no commissions on the transaction since it was my loan. In essence the corporate office did the loan and did so at a fair price. However, these again were expenses I was forced to bear greater than customary fees. One would think problem solved, right? All of the fraud cleaned up, accounts closed resulting from fraud or had fraudulent activity, right? Wrong! You see, this only put a Band-Aid on the problem and raised expenses dramatically. While the cost to get the loan were reasonable given the credit, they were still fairly large, roughly five thousand dollars in all. Secondly, this caused many accounts that had been opened for many years on my reports to all close at one time. Though they were paid in full this destroyed my credit score that was already badly damaged from the identity theft.

HINT:
Manage the closing of accounts and account types. This will be outlined in a later section. However, I thought at the time the best plan of attack was to alleviate the multiple thousands in expenses that had to be covered weekly. The funny thing is it did not stop them; the fraud continued to occur. In fact, many of the accounts that had been paid off by the closing had balances run up on them even though the accounts were closed. If you do not think this can happen let me tell you it can. What they do is they close an account with a balance but interest, late fees, penalties, etc. continue to accrue and it snowballs. The thing was I was not even aware this was occurring on these accounts.

The first closing occurred in September 2006 and took my house payment from $600 monthly to over $900 monthly and still did not solve the problem. So I was forced to refinance again 3-4 months later. However, the second closing was done using a real bottom feeder firm, as my firm could not do the second refinance. I was faced with no choice in the matter as by this stage many of the accounts that were the result of fraud had acquired default judgments when I was not even aware of them, which is yet another thing we will discuss in a later chapter. The second closing was outrageous in fees, nearly $10,000 once you factor in the prepayment penalty from the first loan. To make matters worse by the time I paid the fees, new insurance and tax escrow I barely cleared a little over $5,000 in actual cash. You say why would you close then, and the answer is simple: I had no choice.

The first loan had closed in September of 2006 was being sold over and over. By the time I actually closed the second loan it had been sold 4 times in a 90-day period. This in itself-created a problem as when the loan was paid off it had to be forwarded to the last loan owner and they then reported me 30 days late on my mortgage. Not only is this incorrect but due to the sale per the original contract they could not report me late for 60 days following each respective sale -- but they did. I spent the next 24 months fighting this single point and after nearly two and half years after the closing I was able to get it fixed as this would continue to report falsely on my report for the next seven years otherwise.

You might think why does it matter and the answer is given the accounts that had been closed and the fraud I had to take measures to try to make the reports as accurate as possible to maintain as high a score as possible and every point matters. Secondly, I hold a securities license and when this is the case you have an annual meeting with your broker dealer vendor every year. When this meeting occurs you have to explain every derogatory item on all records, credit reports, public records (like judgments), civil and criminal records and so on. Since the identity theft in May of 2006, these annual meetings were grueling and most years since the event the meeting required tons of supporting documents to be provided following the meeting so the file could be documented. This factored in even if the same matter had been documented the year before, it still had to be redone again the next year to give the broker dealer an update on the progress of the matter. This is an example of those regulators I mentioned earlier working against you.

Chapter 3
The Creditor Disputes Begin

Bad Foundation

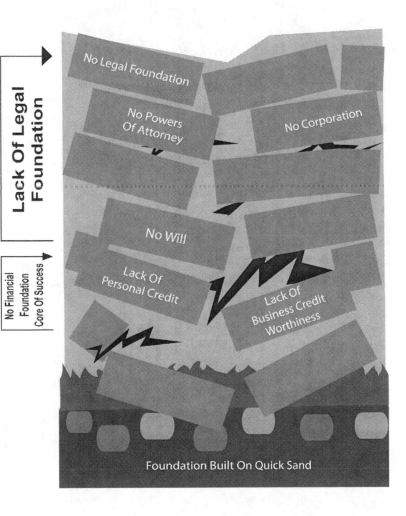

Bad Financial House

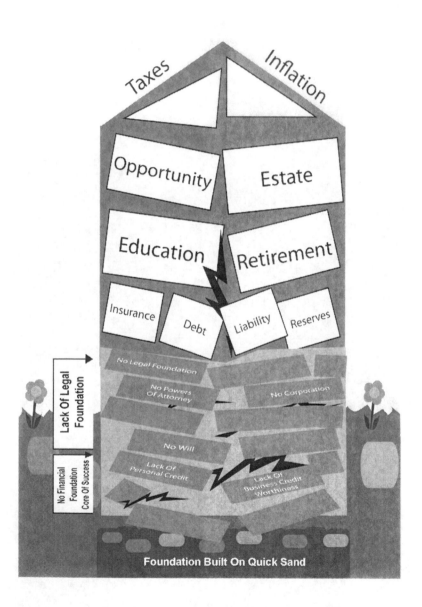

This leads me into 2007. At this stage I am disputing creditors through my legal service on a limited basis, filing disputes with regulators like those listed earlier and many others not listed. The law firm is writing dispute letters disputing literally pages of items by creditor name and partial account number, inquiry and date and so on. Followed by a section referencing the reason for the dispute of each respective item in the next section of the letter. The three primary credit bureaus would investigate these items and they would remove some, claim others as verified and claim to have updated others. This required some items to be re-disputed multiple times. This dispute process was ongoing simultaneously with each respective credit bureau (also known as CRA's, credit reporting agencies).

HINT:
Per the FCRA & Debt Collections Practices Acts there are specific requirements and timelines; if they fail to comply with these the items in question must be removed without exception (see resource section).

These bureaus many times will intentionally ignore their requirements until you force them to comply by being persistent and disputing the items. It is critical that you understand the credit bureaus are not on your side either. You see, the credit bureaus charge the creditors to report to their credit bureaus. Secondly, the credit bureaus sell your information to creditors for marketing purposes and those with the less than perfect credit are not only marketed to the most but charged the highest interest rates and fees. Which means the creditors buying these marketing lists make even more money. In the past, in many states government officials had passed what were called usury laws or caps on what can be charged. However, in many of the states these laws have been watered down and literally repealed in some states allowing the creditors to charge whatever amount they want with no limit whatsoever. This is a second example of those protection agencies working against you through the interpretation and amendment to the laws they enforce and doing so at the direction of the very people they regulate.

You might ask why would the officials do this and the answer is simply campaign contributions and PAC money (Political Action Committee contributions). PAC's are essentially the lobbying groups established to represent industries like the banking industry, insurance industry and so on. You might also ask how am I familiar with this and I think it is critical you understand that I am aware of this as I used to be on the board of NAIFA (National Association of Insurance and Financial Advisers) in Michigan. However, within the board were a number of subcommittees and among these various committees is an organization called **PAC/PIC** committee (Political Action Committee/ Political Involvement Committee). Yes, I was one of them, and that's why I know how they operate. However, before you shut off your ears to what I have to say know that I did it for the sole purpose of gaining inside information on their operations.

While actions like repealing usury laws are morally reprehensible by any standard, on the flip side many other organizations were trying to pass laws that were not in the best interests of the citizens either. One such example in the insurance business has been under the government's constant attack: to allow death benefits from life insurance to be taxable. To this day they are not with a few minor exceptions primarily within the business realm. Without these evil lobbyists life insurance proceeds would be fully taxable and would overnight evaporate the industry, as no one would buy life insurance, since this is one of the primary reasons it is sold. This could be said for any number of industries whether it is the automotive industry, the building industry, you name it and there is a lobbyist group. I left the group once I gained my inside information and began lobbying against them, even though I am both an insurance and securities professional, when they passed the disturbing law that allows property and casualty agents to charge clients higher premiums based on their credit score.

At one of these board meetings a property casualty agent and myself actually got into an argument that almost came to blows as I called the action corrupt. He said the correlation between credit score, claims and rates was easily seen and I told him there are many people who have never had a claim but have a low credit score for another reason. It was at this point that I resigned from the board and NAIFA altogether. I then made my departure very public so all of my clients and the general public knew what they stand for. While the organization may have done some good things they did some corrupt things as well, much like the CRA's we were talking about earlier but they are worse.

Now that I have given you a primer in lobbyists and touched on CRA's let me return to the story. I will pick this conversation up again as later you will see its importance to your long-term fight in recapturing your identity. As I mentioned earlier we are now into 2007, roughly seven months since the identity theft and little did I know the storm had not even come close to hitting yet. You see I had hired two organizations to help me with two very important pieces of the identity theft recapture and I am not passing judgment on these two industries specifically but will pass judgment on the vendors that I selected within these two industries. You do not need to hire vendors of this nature unless you desire to but I had no more time; I had no choice. I literally had no more time. I was using my 24 hours a day as much as humanly possible. It was not uncommon for me at this stage to get two or three hours of sleep a night or a few minutes at my desk and most Saturdays I crashed and here is why.

You may remember my one partner suggested that we take out the other investors and we did this. However, at the last minute he asked me to allow his son to join us to make it the three of us. I thought why not, the more money less problems I would have. So between 2004 and 2006 we eliminated all investors and acquired $3.8 million on a constantly turning basis in real estate and wanted more.

In order to prevent dilution of profits we also set up a realty firm, a 501(c)3 and a limited partnership. The thought behind this was the following: I secured my real estate broker's license so I could handle our transactions, as in our state after a certain number of real estate transactions broker representation was required. Secondly, because foreclosures were on the rise in Michigan, there were a number of grant programs to aid organizations like ours to take control of these properties and get them income and tax paying again. Finally, the limited partnership allowed only outsiders with deep pockets (sophisticated and accredited investors only) to participate but for us to maintain control and place them as a passive investor.

As you may recall my partners were fully aware of my identity theft and knew I was swamped with legal challenges as a result. They knew this would aid me in terms of an influx of cash in my holding company, but in reality they were setting the stage to fleece me. This approach worked through the end of 2007. However, by late 2007 the partners were looking for even higher returns and at this stage in the Michigan economy the real estate market was overheating due to excessive growth and appreciation, and the pendulum was about to swing the other way and I recognized this. I told them we needed to hunker down and brace for a swing but that we needed to continue to grow, though being more selective in the deals. The partners took this to mean buy no more deals and by the end of 2007 they wanted to sell everything, which was the worst decision they could have made both from an economic standpoint but also financially for my identity theft battle. We disbanded the entities and returned all investor funds and required profits. I then set up my group of entities in the same capacities, except the limited partnership, as my approach was to be somewhat different in that I formed smaller partnerships to acquire larger properties. These continue to exist today.

You see, as with investing you can not always run when things get tough and dealing with identity theft is much the same way. Rather than dealing in credit to fund my businesses I brought in private investors (OPM, other people's money) for a specific property, some for a specific entity and so on. All while this was going on I was still battling my identity theft using my selected vendors. Now that you know what was going on during this period of time let me tell you about the vendors I hired, as they changed over time.

First, back in 2004 when I secured my agreement with the legal service, their marketing firm also offered an identity theft protection product. The basics of the product was an insurance policy underwritten by a company that will remain nameless only because I do not want to be sued as they are a corrupt organization to say the least (and that is being polite) and I am currently suing them. You see, this vendor received just under $10 a month every month until my claim was filed in 2006. I then submitted expenses that were to be reimbursed under the policy, much like if you had an insurance claim on your house less the deductible. The policy was to cover such items as legal reimbursement for attorney's fees, court costs, postage, and lost wages up to four weeks at a rate not to exceed $500 per week for said four weeks based on your tax return. The policy was to essentially reimburse me for out-of-pocket expenses incurred as a result of the identity theft.

They initially opened the matter and right out of the gate tried to deny some covered expenses but paid others. I then submitted further documentation on the denied items and some were covered and some were denied again. We went back and forth and I gathered expenses and submitted them in batches every few months. In 2008 a claim was made for some more of the four weeks of time off work and was paid but they began the real injustice at this stage. You see, when the claim was filed in 2006 they paid me the initial two weeks off at the cap rate of $500 per week and when I submitted the second group of time they tried to pay me $200 total for the two weeks. They claimed I was self-employed, which was absolute garbage as I had always been self-employed. Nothing had changed. What they did in the calculation was omitted my entire K-1 which is like a W-2 for the self-employed and only used things like my 1099 for interest paid on my home loan and similar items. This was simply one example of injustice.

Then they tried to deny reimbursement of expenses for legal services by the provider firm that did my legal letters (attorneys) because the claim was part of my legal membership, which had no impact on the policy in question even if that were true -- which it actually was not. After fighting with them over a number of these items I finally got fed up and turned the matter over to my legal service and asked them to prepare a letter to address the issue. This was when the true political fallout of my identity theft really hit the fan and here is why. You see, I was asking my legal service to write a letter to the insurance company handling my identity theft policy protection but the same company marketed both the legal service and the identity theft protection. The marketing company in essence gave the legal firm their marching orders and they intentionally tanked this letter.

I called the legal service and asked them to outsource it to an outside firm given the legal conflict of interest. They bounced it around form firm to firm but it was never handled. While this was all going on the relationship with the main provider firm for my legal service had deteriorated quickly. They began finding reasons to deny me services on unrelated matters and it got to a point where we hated each other and I filed formal charges against one of the law firm partners with the Michigan Bar Association. However, the marketing firm, given its clout as it has provider firms in all fifty states, called the Bar in the provider firm's behalf and essentially got the matter swept under the rug. I appealed but by this stage the matter was dead. I was being overrun by politics.

I then called the marketing firm's corporate office and demanded they assign my account to an alternate provider firm, as the provider firm after I filed action against its partners would not handle my matters even though I was a paying member. Moreover, frankly, given the situation I did not want them handling other matters of mine. So the firm agreed to run my requests through corporate and would assign them to an attorney that handled the type of law in question and would pay them as they had done for the provider firm. However, as you may recall I was disputing literally pages of items at a time and all of these matters after nearly three months had to all be reassigned through corporate. I then had to re-forward to the new assigned attorney all of the same items previously submitted on each. This process took several months and began in July 2008, greatly slowing my progress on things. Fortunately, an executive at the corporate office understood my plight and began working diligently to get things reassigned by the end of November 2008.

However, the problem then was that many of the attorneys assigned to the matters in question did not handle the types of law involved on the respective matters, forcing many to be reassigned multiple times, some two and three additional times. Nonetheless, we then began making headway again. By this time we were into 2009 and throughout that year I was submitting the individual matters in groups of five at a time or so and we began getting things removed gradually from each of the credit bureaus. But by spring of 2009 we were faced with yet another bottleneck because the agents in the corporate assignment office were not paying close enough attention to the types of law and were faced with another bottleneck of matters that had to be reassigned. To prevent this from happening again, we instituted an e-mail system by which I outlined the type of matter, the creditor and the executive involved. We then had it assigned to an appropriate attorney. We were back on track again but had to unclog the bottleneck and in this process several referral attorneys got upset, as they were not paid because of the bottleneck and matters were reassigned to an attorney who got them handled. This created even more political fallout as referral attorneys then began to deny handling my matters. But over the next month I was able to put together a list of five or six attorneys that were part of the network that were effective, efficient and consistent at handling the matters.

*_HINT:_
Whether or not you use a legal service or have a firm on
retainer you need to create a list of attorneys that handle the
following areas of law. This is only a basic list and you may
find that you need a few additional categories specific to your
situation.

- FCRA attorney
- Contract law & collections attorney
- civil action attorney

*This will be explained in more detail in a later chapter and a
process will be outlined so that by the time you complete this
book you will have your legal team formed.

Before you think all things were swell with this vendor you
need to know that I was unjustifiably denied assistance on more
than 10 matters by the legal service that were covered between
2007 and the present. This legal service relationship eventually,
as of a few weeks ago, was terminated. This termination was
by them rescinding their agreement. They took this approach
after I caught the previously mentioned executive attempting
to breach the attorney client privilege and now I am faced with
taking action against the legal service as well.

HINT:
Legal services like this are fine but be sure you know the
contract inside and out and that you are given service that
is effective and timely, as time is of the essence when dealing
with identity theft. Also be sure to use a service that offers an
unlimited number of matters, otherwise you are wasting your
money.

Many legal services are like this. I have not mentioned this
vendor by name as the purpose of this book is to educate,
not promote a particular company. The vendor, given the
events directly above, may be sued for the 10 prior breaches
and attempts to breach the attorney client privilege that they

forced me to endure. I realize to the layman this may sound both petty and vicious, and you are correct as the firm in question was paid for a service that was not completely or satisfactorily fulfilled. When you deal with identity theft you can not overlook matters of this type. You have to be hyper technical and formalities matter, as you will learn in greater detail in subsequent chapters.

A second vendor I hired in late 2006 and eventually fired roughly fourteen months or so later was what is commonly referred to as a credit repair firm. With firms of this nature you pay them a small retainer fee and then pay them a fixed amount monthly to dispute matters on your behalf. When I selected this firm my thought was that with them fighting the disputes, being a legal firm, and my legal service fighting creditors individually, more ground would be covered faster and this was true at the time. However, many times this meant me submitting packages to them both regularly and that was very time-consuming, though as they both got rolling 2007 seemed like it was going to turn out to be very effective. When I signed up with the firm in question they told me to expect the clean up to take roughly 12 months.

The twelve-month mark came and went and things had been removed but nowhere near done. They told me that surely in a few months I would be all set, though my credit due to the theft was exceptionally bad. At the end of each year the firm sends you a packet of all of the communications for the prior 12 months in a box. I started looking at them and realized why I was not further along than I was. By mid to late 2007 I had terminated them. I did this, as they did not even put the letter on legal letterhead or cite the case law that had been violated. I thought if this was all they are going to do I could do this better than they could.

I began searching the Internet concerning case law and learned that the Debt Collections Act and Fair Credit Reporting Act (FCRA) were the backbone of the disputes. While there are other relevant laws that apply from matter to matter these were the common threads to them all. I then began researching other firms like the prior firm to take their place, as I did not have the time or the knowledge to take this on. Remember, I was running my insurance practice, securities practice, and the mortgage company, which by this time had more than 200 loan officers working underneath me. I also had the realty firm and the property company that I outlined before, and I had to keep all investors informed on an ongoing basis. This was all on top the countless battles noted thus far that I continued to wage. I was getting merely 3-4 hours of sleep at night as it was, and I had no more time to give as I was already working at this pace seven days a week.

I then came across a firm that had sample letters to be used as a guide for filing dispute claims yourself. This seemed like a no brainer to me as my thought was though I did not have the time, it would truly save me both time and money in the long run. I pulled the trigger when I realized I would only be doing one dispute with no more than five items in dispute per bureau roughly every 30-45 days with some exceptions to be outlined in a later chapter. You essentially did a single dispute to each of the credit bureaus.

This was by far one of the best decisions I ever made. You see, this put me in control of the letters and when I received a response I could react very swiftly and harshly effectively. This is the mind-set you must have with this: be hyper technical from how the letter is sent, when sent, what is included in each respective letter, time to respond and so on. Per the FCRA, the creditors have specific requirements that must be included in their response, how gathered, time to respond and so forth. If even one thing is missed the item has to be removed without exception.

HINT:
Only use proven letters, as ambiguity is your enemy in a dispute letter (modified samples I have created from scratch and have used in resource section).

* These samples came from attorneys that have written letters on my behalf but have redacted particulars (law firm, account #'s, etc. for privacy reasons)

I then started looking at some of the letters that had been done previously by the legal service to creditors and I also saw similarities and specific sections of laws cited during similar instances. I started using these past letters as templates as well in 2009 & 2010 consistently and really began to make headway on things.

* DO NOT HOLD YOURSELF OUT AS A LEGAL PROFESSIONAL BUT DO CITE THE LAWS THAT ARE PUBLIC INFORMATION. MAKING YOUR KNOWLEDGE OF THEIR VIOLATION KNOWN IS KEY TO AN EFFECTIVE LETTER RESULT.

Good Foundation

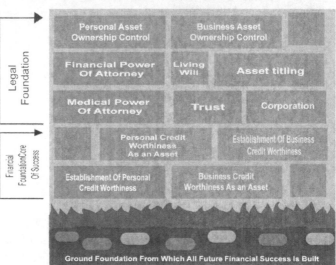

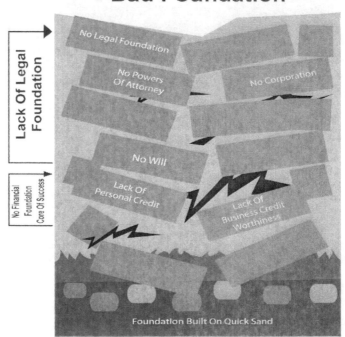

Chapter 4
Treatment Like a Criminal After Doing Nothing Wrong

Now, returning to the story, while all of this was going on I was submersed in business things and dispute things. However, an event would happen in 2007 that would change my outlook on things like no other. I was stopped for a traffic violation and arrested on a false outstanding felony warrant. I knew this was an error but it launched one of the largest battles of them all. You see, when my identity was stolen attempts were made to do things in my name that were not actually done by me. This caused false felonies to be reported under my record. I enlisted the assistance of my U.S. Congressman and he was able to get these removed relatively quickly as they were not mine. However, this did not occur until the state police, NCIC, FBI and Secret Service did an investigation and the items were found to not belong to me. The items were eventually removed in 2007. End of story, right? Wrong. The items kept reappearing, they were repeated more than four times and continue to happen frequently. Therefore almost annually I am forced to deal with this matter of the false felonies being reinserted in error. You may also remember I stated earlier that the entire process was politically charged and it is.

Several state agency officials were found guilty of misconduct and they kept using the initial false insertion to cause me hardship. I ended up in 2009 contacting several of the officials stated earlier to deal with the matter and got nowhere. So in 2010 I was forced to lodge a legal challenge regarding the matter. It now involved numerous government agencies, circuit and district judges, several elected officials, as well as a number of agency employees for willful misconduct and malicious and tortuous conduct, and civil rights violations among other claims. Again I have left their names out due to the pending legal matter. It is underway in federal court having moved its way through the entire state court system all the way to the Michigan Supreme Court due to the political and governmental agencies involved.

The case made its way into federal court in mid-2012. However, the presiding judge prior to his current appointment had been chief judge for the state jurisdiction involved. As chief judge he supervised all of the employees accused of misconduct and oversaw the state personnel involved. So one would obviously expect him to recuse himself due to blatant conflict of interest and bias that no one could overlook. You would be wrong. In fact, in a recusal hearing to get him removed from the case the court allowed him to preside over his own recusal! He went on the record and outlined the fact that he worked in a supervisory capacity in the state judge jurisdiction listed in the complaint. This man had worked for many years at the same law firm with one of the defendants prior to becoming chief judge of the state court jurisdiction in question. Surely this would be ground for recusal. He ruled otherwise; what a shock.

I then had to file a motion of recusal, appeal, etc. and this initiated yet another battle as this federal judge and his underling federal judge proceeded to try to offer political cover and flat out ignore the law. They used unrelated laws in perverse manners to try to get the case dismissed. After spending all of 2011, 2012 and early 2013 battling motion after motion after appeal the case was dismissed. However, it is being appealed in federal appeals court and it is expected that the federal appeals case will be heard in Ohio federal court of appeals sometime in late 2013 or early 2014.

However, this is not the whole story you see. Once I filed the suit against the state personnel, I followed it up with complaints to numerous state and federal regulators including the Michigan administrative supreme court, grievance court with the state of Michigan, the Judicial Tenure Commission, Civil Rights Commission, the Michigan bar, attorney general, Federal Trade Commission... The list goes on and on. A separate battle had to be waged in each case. Now when I walk into my local county court house I am refused service and actually had unrelated cases that were properly filed in this county court endure numerous civil rights and procedural violations. There were also court clerks acting as judges and far too many violations to list them all, as it would literally take an entire book to expose them all, which I am contemplating. As of this writing this battle is still being waged on these unrelated cases of misconduct and may result in yet another round of federal lawsuits against the county, city, state of Michigan and countless other parties. If this is required federal authorities will be brought in and criminal action will be sought.

I then brought this corruption to the local newspaper and they have tried to further the political cover up and in spite of documented facts they have refused to act on the story. In fact, they have gone on the offensive against me making numerous false statements about me trying to discredit me. As a result as of early September 2013 a group of private citizens who have all been enduring countless acts of misconduct and denial of justice have banded together and have begun yet another group of complaints against the related parties. The judge that frivolously denied justice on these unrelated matters has had complaints filed against him and the court clerks and related court personnel have had complaints filed against them for such acts as practicing law without a license and countless other claims. These disputes have been submitted to the proper authorities and are awaiting action. If action is not received the group is prepared to take the matter to Washington federal court regulators. In an effort to keep the pressure on the situation a letter and editorial campaign has begun and is being sent around to numerous media forms from newspapers, TV news, etc. on the national stage. This is all in an effort to expose the corruption that is present within this prominent Michigan county government and turn to unbiased media venues.

It is critical that when you are dealing with identity theft that you be polite and diplomatic but do not let this need be overrun by blatant misconduct. This happens at all levels of government, believe me, I know first-hand from experience as a government intern as well as an identity theft victim. Managing this balance is probably the most emotionally challenging part of the entire process.

You have seen previously the complaints to agencies like the Michigan Bar Association, the FTC for misconduct on the part of creditors, and numerous others that I have cited earlier in this book (and those that have not been specifically outlined). The truth is, I could write an entire separate book just on the malfeasance of the various people involved in this ordeal. I do feel it is worth mentioning though that the majority of the corruption and malfeasance from a percentage perspective has taken place at the state level and the state's various agencies and personnel. This in no way absolves the federal participants as they are guilty of such actions as well but the majority by far occurred at the state level. Additionally, most of the errors at the federal level are on the part of the federal agencies' personnel not the liaisons that oversee them. However, I could even cite a few examples in this regard as well. I am bringing these points up because it is critical that you manage this situation very closely, as it will greatly impugn your efforts if you fail to manage this injustice factor effectively. I realize it is very hard for the layman to understand that officials you elected and the agencies that report to them would intentionally cause you harm but they do and here are a few simple reasons why.

This helps them make the case for greater funding for their department. Various agency employees form opinions as to who should be helped based solely on many arbitrary things that have no relevance to the matter at hand. It could be something as simple as they decide they do not want to help you even though you are entitled to the assistance and assistance is warranted. Another is each agency oversees multiple areas of specialty and if your matter is not in an area they are most concerned about it may suffer; even if an area they cover is simply not at the top of their priority list your request may fall on deaf ears. It comes down to the saying the squeaky wheel gets the grease. However, this persistence will sometimes be met with resistance so be prepared. This is why managing the balance between persistence and obnoxious obsession is a very fine line... far finer than one can imagine.

I can tell you from experience that you have to push the envelope in this regard and here is why. We are talking about your credit report, your reputation, and your sense of character and no one should have authority to arbitrarily substitute their judgment in this regard. Your identity is specific to you and once damaged it can take a lifetime to correct if you do not handle these matters promptly and sternly, as falsehoods present for long periods of time can potentially develop a sense of legitimacy even if they are blatant lies. Because of this fact you must not take your credit report errors as a passive matter. The average person has more than 50% of his/her information incorrect in some fashion within their reports and various trade line items. With a track record like that I find it astonishing to me that the government does not hold them to a higher standard than they do. Here is what I would say. The government has set the standard, it's the law, but it is your job to hold them to the standard and enforce the law.

The story continues throughout early 2007 with disputes being filed with the various CRA's, creditors, legal suits and so on. While this was a very time-consuming process and progress was slower, the battles, when won, were somewhat larger victories. However, each time I solved one challenge a new one would develop. I began to feel like a hamster on a wheel that would not stop. Then in May of 2007 another personal challenge developed. You remember the source bank where the theft originated? I was still dealing with theft but they reached an all-time low. You see, I had inserted my funds to cover my mortgage payment that I had sent to the creditor by check and the check bounced. Here is the ironic part. The mortgage company actually got the money but claimed they did not. I went to a branch and they verified through transaction numbers that the funds left my account when the mortgage company presented the check through an electronic check reader. This started a whole new challenge. I had originally tried to make my payment by phone but the mortgage company's electronic payment by phone service was acting up and I did not receive a confirmation number. I then called the mortgage company's customer service department and they assured me the payment did not go through and instructed me to mail it and that I would not be late if I sent it overnight, so I did. However, it turns out it did go through so they tried to take out two payments when actually only one was made.

When this became known a formal investigation had to take place and they told me not to worry they would correct the situation. The mortgage company sent me back the second payment so I could square up with my bank. However, they did not reimburse the bank charges that resulted or the other checks that bounced as a by-product of this event. I then made another payment for the next month and learned that a new problem had developed with the mortgage company. When they sent back the over-payments they were to reverse the second payment but they reversed both payments but kept one. This essentially meant I paid one but they showed none was paid even though I have a letter from the bank proving this occurred. I called the customer service department again and this process kept repeating itself and they then tried to report me for what is called a rolling 30 day late on the mortgage when all payments had actually been received. I had the legal service send a letter addressing the matter but this only shut off communication altogether.

I then called the customer service department and they told me to escrow payments until we got the matter resolved, but then later refused to accept these payments and threatened to put me in default status. I then had the legal service send another series of letters, the first relating to the false reporting on the credit bureaus in terms of latest and the second the threat of default even though all payments were made. They eventually started the default process in late 2007 and even though I had the funds they would not accept them. I will outline shortly why this was. However, I continued on with this battle throughout 2007 and into 2008. In February 2008 they started foreclosure proceedings due to the payments not being received only because they would not take them. I tried to mail multiple cashier checks by overnight mail and they were all returned. The home went into the redemption period and was officially lost on August 22, 2008 following the end of the redemption period. For those who are not familiar with this term the redemption period is when a loan goes into default status and the owner is given six months to bring things current. However, remember I was trying to mail said payments and they would not accept them. This process will vary greatly from state to state. This is another example of those consumer protection affiliates supposedly looking out for the consumer but truly looking out for those they monitor.

Keep in mind that politics played a big factor in the identity theft and the matters surrounding it. They did not want me to redeem my house because I had just completely renovated and re landscaped it before the identity theft occurred. The bank seized the property and claimed to have sold it for less than half of its actual value and sent me a 1099 for the difference. This 1099 was for over $60,000. I had the legal service send another group of letters relating to the house to the former mortgage company addressing the following items. First the falsely issued 1099 as they sold the home to one of their affiliates and held it for the minimum amount of time and then sold it for a huge profit. The second item was the false reporting under the Debt Collections Practices Act, FCRA and numerous unethical and malicious actions. To paint the picture more clearly let me cite one example of their egregious actions. The utilities were physically shut off in December 2007 and I paid the final bill. However, the former mortgage company "encouraged" shall we say that the utilities be charged to me for all of 2008 when I was not even present or the utilities even on. This would make it impossible for me to get utilities in my name elsewhere and I had to fight this battle with consumers once again. I will devote a later chapter entirely to Consumers Energy, as there is no more corrupt organization than this utility company that has a monopoly in this region of Michigan. While up until this point

I have not named any creditors by name this is one creditor that has warranted an exception.

From a credit standpoint the mortgage matter was by far the worst because it hit things on many fronts. One, it affected my credit and related score with the falsehoods and the eventual false foreclosure, thus defrauding me out of my home, its equity and the reporting of this in public records even though none of it was actually true. They simply would not accept the payments.

You may also recall that I am security licensed and as I referenced previously there is an annual meeting with my broker dealer. It was rather hard to claim I was cleaning up the identity theft (though I was) when things like the mortgage matter were still occurring. This year the annual filing was so grueling it literally took six meetings by conference call and numerous follow-ups in writing.

I should also back up and reference the fact that the reason the mortgage company wanted my house was because oil was discovered across the street and they had purchased all of the surrounding houses and needed mine to lock things up. The chain of events got so bad that everyone knew what occurred to me, which compelled nearly every person at the end of the street to sell -- as they knew if they did not they were next. Remember this point as it will have much greater meaning when we get to the chapter devoted to consumers energy. To my joy their long-term plans in this regard were shot down because there was a river in close proximity. This was a small victory of retribution. However, they had still reaped a financial windfall on the resale of my home having stolen it from me for pennies on the dollar.

2007 was by far the roughest year of the identity theft. Every day new unknown challenges emerged that would need to be dealt with for many months into the future. You see, in 2007 I had to renew all the insurance and securities licenses, continuing education and so on. But in doing so I had to once again, in a far more aggressive and detailed manner explain the entire identity theft matter creditor by creditor to avoid losing my livelihood. I submitted all of my continuing education documentation and the state personnel sat on my items until the day after my renewal. This led to all of my carriers dropping me and I lost all of my renewals. Even though it was fixed one week later I was now out of all of my prior renewals. This event destroyed me financially, as I lost my office due to all of the built up revenue that supported this building (where my office was located) and its daily costs. The entire process was started and finished the last half of the year. This happened before my default on my house. I still had all of my licenses but none of my vested renewals.

I began to liquidate assets from companies and personal assets from my muscle car collection and all home furnishings. I used these proceeds to keep my licenses and then when the foreclosure redemption started I knew I had to liquidate all and this was when I eliminated my partners and sold all remaining items including my Explorer XLT. The irony of this was that the week before the sale the motor locked up and would not run. It is believed that this was messed with and I am confident I know who did this but the police found no prints except for mine. However, I used my last $35 dollars and placed an ad to run a major sale at the house. I sold everything, appliances, remaining paint supplies, furniture, clothes, everything. When this was all done I cleared just under $9,000 as these items were sold at fire sale prices to ensure liquidation. I then used a small portion to acquire a couple new business outfits, a luggage case and establish my current entities with the only old remaining entity being my holding company that held my insurance and securities practices. I then sold my clients in all divisions and used these funds to establish a formal business plan for each division's new entities that would replace those held with the partners as previously outlined.

I found myself sleeping on the floor in the house with no heat, electricity or water for nearly a month in December and had to walk to everything. I used my time to write the general outline of the various divisions and the associated business plan outlines.

During the house's redemption period even though I was not present I made sure the house looked lived in by keeping the walk shoveled in winter and through August of 2008 the lawn mowed. You might ask why did I do this? It is simply that I needed to keep the redemption period open the entire six months. You see, if you just leave they only have to give you 30 days and I was not fully sure yet if the home was going to be redeemed or not. Secondly, I felt I owed it to my neighbors to not have the house looking abandoned.

The entire year of 2007 could have been seen as a negative one given all of the battles that were waged, the loss of the office and the beginning of the default period on the house. However, I found the event liberating in that it allowed me to sell everything and start fresh. I started with the office by liquidating the office furniture and the various client bases. I then moved onto the home furnishings, clothes and other items. Finally, I liquidated appliances and everything else. Most people saw this process in a favorable light because I presented it as such. Remember I told you emotional attitude is a very big part of this overall process.

In terms of the identity theft clean up a great deal of accounts were removed from the various credit bureaus. This process really began to move once I fired the one vendor that was previously handling this, as I have already stated.

This moves us into 2008. I would call it the year of preparation of the new beginning of the rebuilding process on many fronts. The entire year was focused on the following areas: government agency submissions and the forcing of these agencies to do their job, continuing the removal of the fraudulent accounts, the ongoing battle with the source bank, and the addition of accounts that previously were not reporting. Furthermore, I was working with the plan writers to compile the formal business plans for each division with fully prepared CPA financials and began the funding process.

The first two or three months were spent working on these but it took me this initial group of months to wind down from working 20 hour days, as once all the divisions were sold the days were dramatically cut in length. This did not mean there was not plenty to do but it meant I could do so on a more traditional schedule. It took me the first three months before I could stop waking up after only three hours or so of sleep. I found myself waking up and working on getting things done. I had to force myself to readjust my schedule. However, the initial three months I got considerable amounts done because of the adjustment period. The second two or three months of the year most of the rough drafts of the business plans, financials and alike began to come together. I then hired a grant writer and a formal plan writer to take these rough drafts and put them into a more formal form that could be used by the funders and the grant writer. I put the grant writer on retainer and she began to supposedly work on things. You will find that once you have been a victim of identity theft you are exposed to more scoundrels. The first grant writing firm I hired after nearly six months basically got a great deal of money but made very little progress. I eventually was forced to fire them and take them to court and received a partial refund. However, the time was lost and this could not be mistaken. I by this time had the first division's formal plan together and the plan writer and I began working on the others. Being that the first took roughly 4-6 months to complete I figured the others would go very quickly as they were based on the initial plan. This could not be further from the truth. The process took another eight months or so, 14 months in all to complete.

By this time I had located another grant writer and began submitting these plans to her so she could begin locating the grant funds and the funders could fund the difference. However, after another 12 months this grant writer had nearly been paid in full but was not far along as in fact many of things she had done needed fixing and I am still cleaning up this mess.

I am currently suing this grant writer as we speak. I cannot stress enough that once you have become a victim of identity theft you are exposed to twice as many people who are out for a quick buck. I bring this up because it is critical that you remain conscious of this fact while trying to put things back together. At times this will make you come off very jaded and it will be your need to monitor this so as to not make yourself counter-productive towards your objectives of identity recapture, and professional and financial success following the event.

Chapter 5
Legal Options: the In's and Outs

Disclaimer:
this should not be deemed legal advice but rather a layman's approach and are in no way liable for use of these principles or their related outcomes.

SMALL CLAIMS COURT:

In 2008 a large number of the individual lawsuits began to take place. I do not want to dispense legal advice but one thing I can tell you is it is critical that you manage this area very closely as you will find there are numerous paths to take with any one matter. Having said that, here is what I can tell you in this regard and some of this is common sense and part of this is based on your confidence to plead your own case. It is common knowledge that matters under $3,000- $3,500 are deemed small claims cases and if all you are trying to do is get your money back and it's a small amount of money this might be your best option. If it is over this sum then you will move into district court. You can still represent yourself in this arena as well. It is far less common but it can be done quite effectively. I mention this because if you hire an attorney to represent you on every matter you will go broke early on as I learned the hard way. Even though I had the legal service that offered me a free 20 minute consult on each matter, would review up to 10 pages on any matter and write up to one legal letter on a matter, I still had to manage the situation very closely. I soon realized that I not only had to fight all the battles but manage how they were fought.

This at times was problematic but I found it the best way to handle things. I used the legal service to address the matter if I could and if this was not possible I also made sure I had a firm grasp of my available recourse actions and the basic legal argument on the matter. I then would file in the respective court and present the case myself. Sometimes if the matter was small in nature the other party would not even show up and I won a default judgment. If they did show up then we presented our respective cases to the judge and he ruled. I might point out in this regard that in every case thus far the verdict was ruled in my favor. However, in some instances the other party would file a motion to have the matter moved to district court. They did this so they could hire an attorney to handle the matter on their behalf. I did this myself on a couple of matters when they tried to sue me for the fraudulent charges. Even with this occurring many times I would still represent myself rather than hiring an attorney as it is important to manage the situation and in some instances it was simply both more effective in terms of cost and time to handle the matter myself. After handling the first few cases this way, I began using attorneys only for the more serious matters. The cost varies from region to region. In Michigan for small claims court it costs $25.00 to file and the cost of service could run from $5.00 to $50.00 depending upon whether it is done by certified mail or using a process-server.

DISTRICT COURT:
If I was forced to file in district court the filing fee started at $65 and went up based on the size of the claim and again the cost of service as noted above. I think it is critical that you understand that you must efficiently file these claims and doing so on multiple matters in the same jurisdiction is a good idea as long as you can handle appearing on more than one matter in a single day. This will minimize the actual number of days in court and allow you to use your time more efficiently. However, it is critical that you manage this properly as you do not want two court days to end up on the same day in two different towns and this can happen as it happened to me. It is also important to file matters strategically. Sometimes filing related matters together is good, but other times it is not. This is a trial and error situation that you must feel out for the region in question. In certain cases it is better to make sure that similar matters are not heard on the same day as the tainting of one matter can taint them all. Also this will impact the judge you draw on the respective matters. Sometimes getting the same

judge for related matters is a plus while other times it is not. Again you have to monitor this closely during your supervision of the process.

Some matters will require to be handled in civil court. This is where you are seeking damages in addition to the reimbursement or correction of a particular issue. I have had very little experience thus far in this realm as it was suggested to me to handle things in the following order to build up the supporting claims on a matter that may end up in civil court. This means handling the small claims matters, then those of the district court, followed by the federal court and finally the civil matters. However, you must also manage your timeline as some matters have statutory timelines that you must comply with and over time you may have matters occurring in each of the courts at the same time. We have not covered the federal courts yet but we will. I am saving this for the last part of the court discussion, as this is where a large portion of the credit disputes will be waged.

COURTS IN GENERAL:
Returning to our conversation in terms of small claims and district courts. As I said earlier some creditors that have been defrauded by the people who have stolen your identity will try to haul you into court and secure a judgment. If they are successful there may or may not be recourse to be taken. If it is in small claims there is no recourse unless you can show it was result of fraud and if this is required you very well may have to hire an attorney. If this is a solid fear with a particular creditor, when you receive the notice have the matter moved to district court and hire an attorney. However, the upside of this is that it uncaps the amount of the judgment that can be entered if it is ruled against you so this is a double-edged sword that you must be aware of. Never fail to appear at a hearing or they will rule against you for certain. You may remember I said this process is politically charged so select where to file very carefully within your region, as some courts are more liberal or conservative as the case may be from one to another within the same area and by matter of topic.

Secondly, given the location of the parties involved reduces the choices to a mere handful of options. Finally, which court type should you choose? Small claims, district, civil, or federal court. Most of the conversation thus far has been directed at small claims as it is quick, easy and cost-effective but there will be times when you cannot or do not want to risk the decision being final. You then elect to file in district court and depending on your confidence to present your case you may or may not want to hire a lawyer. What you need to understand is that in some instances if you elect to hire a lawyer you may not recoup all of your legal costs, as the fees in some instances are statutory in nature. If your legal fees exceed these, as they often do, you will be paying these costs and that is OK in some cases. As you will learn, sometimes the importance of winning is more crucial than the costs themselves even if you lose money on the case or break even. Again this comes back to what are the claims and the dollar amounts involved. You must learn early on that you have to fight all battles, and you must do so like a business guy taking into account costs, risks, etc. What little experience I have had in civil court I have found you are typically dealing in very large numbers and it almost always makes sense to have counsel. If you are lacking in money, handle the smaller and simple cases first and then use these proceeds to fund the civil action that you need to file. However, I must stress that you sill have to monitor the statutory time clocks present to file a claim on a matter. I urge you to write these on a calendar so they are not overlooked. I was faced with this only on one matter but it was one that I had simply held off on due to the costs involved even though it was a strong case. You do not want to lose due to the statutory clock timing out.

Though they will be rare, on occasion you will want or need to file motions. These forms are readily available at the court or online; in some instances they are generic forms. However, some courts are fussy in this regard so be sure to get the particulars from the court jurisdiction involved. There is one thing I can tell you about motions and other filings outside of the primary filing. The goal is to minimize this to manage the costs. However, if a motion will put things strongly in your favor do not be afraid to take the time to do this or be cheap in this regard. Again this will vary by region, matter and motion type but can range $3.00 to $100.00 depending on the matter and motions involved. If you receive a motion, be sure to answer it within the specified time or you may be automatically ruled against by default. This will not always happen. Other times you will simply have to appear in court to address the motion, though some courts, due to the large number, try to handle as much by mail as they can.

HINT:
When responding to a motion or other correspondence be sure to do so by certified mail or process-server. No exceptions. You may need to prove this in the future and this gives you that ability should it be needed later on.

HINT:
Be sure to track everything by calendar so nothing is overlooked as every detail matters.

FEDERAL COURTS:
Now I will move on to federal court for those matters that require legal intervention with laws directly relating to the identity theft or compliance with such laws as FCRA, Debt Collection Act, Equal Credit Opportunities Act and other similar laws. All of these fall within the federal court system. I have represented myself on a couple of matters in federal court and I can tell you it was outright tough. First, most federal judges do not like you not having counsel. Second, some will adjourn until you secure counsel. It will depend greatly on the type of matter and the federal judge, jurisdiction and so forth. If the matter is really large dollar amounts hire an attorney, as most will take the case without a retainer and the filing fee being paid, as when you win they will be able to secure restitution of legal fees. However, in some instances there are statutory limits so be conscious of this. I have personally had these be a problem even with the multiple and complex matters.

If the matters you are handling are a bunch of small but important matters that must be handled in federal court, such as improper payment histories and other similar violations, you can file a single filing and simply name all the parties and the respective grievance. The judge will handle them one by one in a single filing. This may vary by dollar amount and region but in Michigan the cost of this filing is $350 dollars. The attorney gets statutory attorney fees. Many times the attorney will take the case on contingency or a particular percentage contingency if large dollar amounts are involved and or if punitive and compensatory damages may also be awarded in addition to actual damages.

If you find an attorney that you feel will do you well, I would be willing to giving him half the award if winning is of greater importance than the money. While money damages will aid you in winning sometimes the win itself is more important to the long-term battle. As you will learn over time a series of wins relating to identity theft will eventually aid you in making the case in future matters. It's kind of like building the cases based on your successes that led you to the case being decided at the time and depending on the direct relevance can hugely impact the final decision. Federal court is submersed in formality and that is why dealing with the matters as much as possible in the other courts can save both time and money. It can also allow you to deal with one aspect of a matter in one court and then seek other facets in federal court, just not the same matters. You can not be awarded twice on the same specific claim in the matter. However, civil damages and actual damages are not the same things. Just like slander and defamation of character are not the same as being made whole in terms of a dollar amount previously lost due to the fraud. The damage to character has its own value. You must pick your battles, where, when and how to fight them. This is the key. I can tell you this is where the legal service helped me the most early on, as I began to get a sense of where and when and how to handle a violation of my identity. Once I gained this understanding the legal service's role changed and became one to simply help me formulate the grievance to seek, action to be taken on my claims an action plan if you will. This section has been meant to serve as a primer on the courts and how to maneuver them in general terms.

THE FOUR BENEFITS OF SUING UNDER:
THE FAIR CREDIT REPORTING ACT (FCRA):

The FCRA is a powerful tool in correcting some of the most damaging of errors - credit report errors. When furnishers - those who supply or "furnish" information to the credit reporting agencies and/or the credit reporting agencies won't correct false information, you often must sue under the FCRA.

First Benefit - Actual Damages:

If the conduct (mis-conduct) of the furnisher or creditor (the one who gives the information) or the credit reporting agency (Equifax, Experian, Trans Union, etc) has actually harmed you, then the FCRA allows you to recover damages to compensate you for your loss. This loss or damage can be in the form of emotional distress (mental anguish) or it can be loss of a job or loss of a mortgage (i.e. you missed out on a house because of false credit reporting), etc. This ability to be compensated for your actual damages is a very powerful and wonderful tool that can help you piece things back together after suffering through a bad situation with false credit reporting.

Second Benefit - Attorney Fees And Costs:

Sometimes the amount of damages you can recover is not enough to pay for your attorney's fees but Congress has allowed you to recover attorney's fees and costs if you are successful in your case. This is critical to allowing you to hire competent and experienced attorneys. It also provides an incentive for the defendants to settle with you so they do not have to pay high attorney's fees. If the furnisher attempts to drown a plaintiff such as myself in paperwork and motions there is a price to be paid for this egregious attempt to hide their crime (and that is exactly what it is). If it is found to be intentional, additional penalties can be imposed as a direct result.

Third Benefit - Statutory Damages:

If the conduct of the defendants was intentional, then you can receive up to $1,000 per violation in what are known as statutory damages. These are damages that are awarded even if you have not suffered actual damages. Instead these damages are to encourage you to bring suit against law-breakers and to encourage the law-breakers to start following the law.

Fourth Benefit - Punitive Damages:

Similar to statutory damages, if there is willful (or wanton) conduct, the judge or jury can award punitive damages. These damages are to punish the wrongdoer. They are also intended to discourage the wrongdoer and similar companies from doing this same or similar type of misconduct. In the FCRA context, this has been as high as 80 times the amount of other damages awarded but more typically it will not exceed 3-5 times the actual damage award you receive.

The furnishers and credit reporting agencies should always have a chance to correct any errors since you must dispute it first. If they don't correct it after you dispute it . . . particularly if you dispute it multiple times . . . then filing a lawsuit is certainly justified. The FCRA is designed to make it possible for you to recover damages and to punish the wrongdoer if the misconduct was intentional. Attorney fees are also provided so you can hire a lawyer even if you don't have a high actual damage award and to also encourage the law-breakers to quickly resolve cases. Bottom line - the FCRA is very powerful and gives you four important benefits.

ATTORNEYS:

Now I want to talk about attorneys and selecting them. Attorneys are not all created equal. Understanding the type of lawyer you need is the first step in securing the right attorney when one is needed. The first question is what type of law is involved and is there more than one type of law involved. If there is, try to avoid the need for two attorneys by selecting the most well-rounded attorney or an attorney that specializes in the area of greatest priority among the claims. You see, when attorneys attend law school they are taught all types of law but commonly they then select a specialty. They may, however, have someone in their office they will consult behind the scenes on something that they have a question on. This also allows the attorney to be selected in a cost-effective manner, with emphasis on the highest priority items but still addressing the others, too. This approach will be very effective, as all items will be noted in the complaint and the judge will handle the highest priority items first and then address the subsequent items. Many times this is best, as once you win the top items the others will be won by default or will be won and simply the award for them will need to be handled.

Lawyers come in primarily two types: trial lawyers and those who are not. The trial litigator is the one who spends the majority of his time arguing cases in front of judges. These attorneys will have a tendency to be very abrasive and argumentative by nature. If you are seeking a litigator find someone you consider rude, as he will be the best. That's because fights are based on arguments, not on whether he likes you. I use a simple analysis. I meet with an attorney and if I pound him with questions and he fires back or comes off as rude that's the guy I will hire, as I know he is a true litigator. When you are in federal court that's what you want; a litigator. They are strong in formality and will be viewed by the layman as nit-picky. Remember I said that identity theft is a challenge fraught with formality and every little detail matters. However, some litigators only work in civil court and not federal court, so this must be asked. You do not want someone who does not do a lot of federal work, even if a good litigator, if you are going to file in federal court as the battle will be lost in the formalities. I learned this the hard way on a small slam dunk case. Luckily, I was able to turn it around in the end in my favor, but you will not always be that lucky.

The second attorney is what I call a contract attorney. They might have a specific area of specialty but are again strong in what I call general contract law. This is the attorney when you need one to assist you with the district court cases you will use as they will base their arguments on the contract violations or lack thereof. However, if the account is 100% fraudulent then you will want a litigator as this matter belongs in federal court in that instance per the statute of frauds, which is federal law. Again, approaching the legal battle strategically is important. The contract law attorney is also effective when you need a simple letter done on legal letterhead. You would be quite surprised how sometimes the properly worded letter can be effective. However, if you then take the letter and place it on legal letterhead it gains punch in effectiveness. This was one of the first things I learned from the legal service and one of the instances that a legal service can help you with during the recapture process.

I would first deal with the low hanging fruit and get your financial coffers up in amount.

I would then handle the district cases next; first, those you can handle yourself, then those requiring an attorney.

I then would handle the civil and federal cases next by order of priority and statutory clock deadline.

I would set up a separate account or fund for the legal challenges and only use these funds for the following items:

Court filings, motions, retainers, fees for counsel when needed, and package preparation to support these objectives, certified postage, supplies for these packages, credit reports, phone expenses, gas for travel to hearings and related meetings. These will add up, so putting money aside for them avoids the desire to spend the money and allows you to fund things without financing them if this is even possible depending on the damage to your credit. As you receive a court award replenish the account.

Once you have everything under control and cleaned up whatever is left should first go to reimburse initial out-of-pocket expenses. Once you are 100% completed in this process then and only then should the funds be redirected for some other purpose. My suggestion would be to keep a small portion on hand in the fund for at least 12 months to make sure nothing else needs to be redressed, was overlooked or pops up following what is thought to be the end of the identity theft clean up.

ATTORNEY COMPENSATION:

In terms of compensation for attorneys the hourly rate will vary widely by area of law, region of the country and the comp model selected. When it comes to district court cases I always try to get them to take it on contingency if they will. If this is not possible rather than going hourly I suggest that they agree to a set fee for handling the matter. This is more cost-effective for you. Regardless of which of these two options you select make sure that the court filing costs are separate, otherwise they minimize the number of motions and other filings to maintain their profitability on the case. By dealing with this separately you avoid the problem. Also in this regard, require them to take the initial filing out of the retainer and the final bill for filings to be paid at the conclusion of the case regardless of the outcome unless it is based on a contingency. If you elect a contingency, these are to come off the top first and then his percentage taken. These might seem like minor matters but I assure you when large numbers are involved this can add up quickly and when small numbers are involved it can all but eliminate the win financially and actually put you at a loss. This is matter you must learn before you hire your first attorney. I learned this hard way when a single one page letter cost me $375.00 and a month to have it prepared.

In federal court it is much simpler but again you should have a couple of options for the most part. The first is to have the case taken on a contingency fee basis in which the attorney gets a set percentage of the award much like above. The court costs are deducted and the percentage is taken. However, with one twist it is very common for attorneys to be compensated statutory fees on top of the award and court costs. This avoids the need for these items to be deducted from the award. The short answer is this is the best option but be sure you read the retainer agreement closely.

The second option is to elect an hourly rate. I would avoid this at all costs. If the attorney wants this approach I would negotiate a set fee to handle the case and lock this in so it is capped. I personally would do the contingency basis when at all possible. To entice them to take your case, if you have a great deal of confidence in the attorneys winning the case for you as noted above, agree to a higher percentage of the award, but let him eat the expenses. This keeps thing nice, clean and simple and as you receive the award multiply this by this percentage and you get the rest. How generous I am in this manner depends on the case and the attorney.

REPUTATION OF THE FIRM FACTOR:
Lastly in terms of compensation is the reputation of the firm or the attorney specifically. Not all cases need the most expensive attorney in town and in many cases you are paying for the reputation not a better job or higher qualified attorney. In the legal realm there are those that have connections and those who have street smarts. You want to manage this situation like everything else, there is a time for connections to be effective and there is a time for street smarts to be used. The lesson for you here is, do not think that the more you pay the better your results as this is not always the case. When I am looking for an attorney I treat it like a job interview. You are looking for a temporary employee. You should outline what you want them to have or do and what it should cost in your region. Then you should evaluate the strength of your case as a whole from a layman's perspective. Next you need to determine if it is a more common matter in nature or highly specialized, and lastly where are you going to file in terms of court type and city.

Then based on this put others on the short list of attorneys that fit the bill and narrow it down to one. However, let me be clear, do not call 10 attorneys and then pick one. Have a list of five, and pick one. If you get a strong sense on the first or second attorney then hire them unless you have reservations.

Then, complete the entire five calls and make the decision. However, if you elect to do this be up front. You are trying to determine who is the best person for the job. The attorney will respect that, let them sell you on why you should use them and not another attorney. Keep in mind these must be true reasons, not fluff or innuendo. No matter what do not ever let an attorney know who he is up against, as the attorneys know if they have competition or not based on who it is and this will prove problematic if you later hire them in terms of negotiation of costs. When figuring out what five attorneys to call open the phone book to lawyers and go to the section of law categories and look at the firms listed in the area you need help with. Secondly, look at the names and see if you recognize or have worked with them in the past. Lastly, ask others about the category list as more than likely a friend will have done business with at least one of them in the past and will have an opinion. You will then have to decide how much weight to give their opinion. Do not call the state bar as these guys do not work for your interest, though they say they do; they work for the attorneys, that is their lobbying group. However, you can see on their site if an attorney has any complaints, but base your decision on more than this or what law school they graduated from.

Finally, go to the respective courthouse and sit in a few minutes of court by type and see which is commonplace in terms of attorneys in these matters and how they present themselves and obviously if it is a successful strategy. Do not judge the attorney by how they dress but by his demeanor and effectiveness. This also lets you get a flavor for the judges as well. Do not talk and sit in the back for easy exit. This was by far one of the best things I did as it allowed me to know where to file and who the players were in the region in terms of attorneys and judges.

Seeing as we are in the legal vein I want to once again bring up the matter of CRA's (credit reporting agencies). Here we are going to talk about these in greater detail. You see, there are many reporting agencies out there and they are all building reports on you. Some are industry specific to industries like banking, payday loans, check writing and the list goes on. When you are a victim of identity theft it is imperative that you seek these out as some firms operate on a regional basis while others function on a national or international basis. Additionally if you have one piece of wrong information on file this can prevent you from getting loans, checking accounts, pay-day loans or any number of services and when you apply and are denied you might not know why. The reasons they may give you in the notice will tell you that they denied you based on information they acquired from a specific source. You then must contact the source, procure a complete report, review it and dispute any incorrect information. When I say any incorrect information I need this to be taken LITERALLY. You see, if you spell your name every day with a middle initial A but the report does not, this might allow others with similar names or even the same name in another part of the country or even world to have their information show up on your report. Or to not show up as the case may be.

I am going to outline a few of these CRA's, some you will have heard of and others you will have not. There are even more than these so check your region for a more comprehensive list. If the group is a true CRA they are required to comply with such laws as the FCRA, Debt Collections Practices Act, ECOA (Equal Credit Opportunities Act) and numerous other laws. Also, if they reside in one state and you reside in another interstate commerce laws may apply. This is all on top of the industry guidelines specific to the industry in question. However, do not let this scare you off. The idea here is to have a layman's grasp of the general landscape of things. Some sample letters that I will include later on in this book will aid you with this understanding to the extent that you should need, but again should not in any way be deemed legal advice.

However, if a peculiar situation is present seek legal counsel as needed; this book is intended to be a do it yourself perspective. You will have to determine when you are outside your capability and seek legal counsel. The hope is that through this education you can handle the majority of the matters yourself and minimize other costs and time to complete. You should be able to do this by learning what to do and what not to do and learn from my successes and my mistakes. So you do not have to repeat them.

2008 and 2009 were my learning curve in this realm.

Chapter 6
Credit Reporting Agencies at a Glimpse

LISTING OF CRA'S & THEIR INDUSTRIES:
I am going to start with some CRA's, with which you may not be familiar. You see, there are a number of industry specific CRA's. Before you make any requests or file any complaints, be sure to read the resource section fully or you will cause yourself problems later on in terms of future disputes.

PRIMARY CREDIT REPORTING AGENCIES:

- Experian
- Trans Union
- Equifax

These three credit bureaus are the primary CRA's used by most businesses that require access to one's credit. This determines the rate something will cost, the amount of money one can have access to on a monthly basis or how past payments have been made. These three bureaus are many times also used to verify information that may have been submitted within an application. While items reporting on any one of these three bureaus may be submitted to the others this is a less common occurrence by the average consumer. If accounts reporting in good standing do not report to a particular bureau this request can be made in writing. However, in some instances the creditor may not be required to comply with your request.

Additionally, many of these credit reporting agencies have created advanced modeling of their credit reports that allow a potential creditor to emphasize specific variables and reassign them different weights of importance than the standard credit report profile. This practice is by far the most discriminatory, as it allows potential creditors to focus on specific variables and eliminate the importance of others and skew the impact in their favor. This practice allows one to subsequently create a target market and victimize those with specific variables within their credit report. This is one of the most offensive and biased acts the credit reporting agencies have perpetrated recently. It essentially allows creditors to legally discriminate by simply altering the model. This is the primary reason credit reporting agencies were created, to prevent this very situation of inappropriate behavior. At least this is what they would have you believe. The true reality is the long-term plan was to move towards this so they could control things and legally discriminate. While each of the big three CRA's offer these advanced models, only recently have they begun to aggressively develop multiple versions for the purpose of making it so the average consumer does not have a clear picture of the parameters involved. Equifax is the leader in this remodeling development. I urge all to acquire these advanced models periodically to ensure the information in them is accurate as well. It is very common for the traditional report and the modeling version to develop errors in this conversion process. Be prepared to meet resistance in acquiring these advanced reports, but remain persistent in this initiative.

CREDIT REPORTING AGENCIES THAT MAY BE INDUSTRY SPECIFIC BUT CONSUMERS MAY NOT BE FAMILIAR WITH:

Chex Systems:
This CRA is used by banks and credit unions to report losses they have incurred by people in an effort to give other banks and credit unions advance warning so they do not suffer the same fate. However, this organization is one of the worst CRA's of them all. This is why I am starting with them. You see, banks sometimes suffer losses like unpaid overdraft fees, payments they honored but were not made whole, multiple overdraft, fraud, providing false information and the list goes on and on.

However, on a whim they make it so you cannot get a checking account, or a check will not be accepted at retailers due to the automated verification system. If you piss one person off at a bank they will make your life a living hell. Remember as I said before these organizations are there for the industries not the consumer as they claim.

This firm is still in business to this day. I am still fighting them as they blatantly and frequently fail to comply with the FCRA and the Debt Collections Practices Acts among others. When selecting a banking institution I always look for banks that are not part of the Chex Systems, as they are vile. There are numerous banks that do not use services of this nature, or Chex Systems specifically.

In regard to my story with Chex Systems, you may recall I was battling on an ongoing basis with the source banks throughout 2008. I saw the battle coming to a head so I opened a second set of checking accounts at another firm. However, when the theft occurred I ended up having to sue the second banking firm and won. Shortly after this occurred in 2008 the source bank turned me into Chex Systems and I have been battling with them ever since. You see, there were several hundred in bank fees from the identity theft and I refused to pay them. You may recall near the beginning of my story I told you the letter I threw out would come back to haunt me. However, they claimed that the police report was insufficient to resolve the matter. I have been battling ever since this and will go to federal court sometime later this year as it is on the schedule per the calendar I previously mentioned. In the reference section I will provide you with the information to enable you to secure a copy of your Chex Systems report and a sample letter to use in the process. Once you review the report you can then dispute items as needed in the same fashion as the CRA's you are familiar with like Trans Union, Experian and Equifax.

You need to be aware that organizations like this are more than politically charged, but rather corrupt as they base their decisions and content solely on banks and what they submit. So if you upset a bank executive or manager they will try to make your life miserable just for fun so be prepared.

SCAN (Shared Check Authorization Network):
This CRA keeps a report of bad checks and acts of alleged fraud. The organization offers retailers the ability to scan a check and see if the presenter has a bad history or not so they can decide if they want to honor it or not.

I checked my SCAN report and had no history and had no black marks so I have never disputed anything with this firm. However, in the resource section I will provide you with the information needed to procure a copy of your SCAN Report. The letter you will use is the same as the Chex Systems letter but you will insert SCAN and their information along with your required particulars.

Again once you receive report you will denote errors and dispute them as needed like any other CRA.

Telecheck:
This is another firm like SCAN or Chex Systems. Of these CRA's, Telecheck is the least vile but they are all vultures and you need to monitor this closely. It will impact many areas of your life ranging from having a checking account, opening an account, closing an account, cashing a check written to you and many other similar everyday functions. You MUST monitor this equally as closely as the big three credit bureaus.

One key point I need to make with all three of the CRA's listed above is they each have their own guidelines as do the banks themselves that they represent. So what this means is that you have to meet both the CRA's guidelines as well as the bank's guidelines you are working with and there is no rhyme or reason and they will not tell them to you even if you ask. Even though this is a direct violation of the FCRA.

If fraud is present there are a few steps you need to take before you begin filing complaints;

- contact the authorities as outlined at the beginning of my story.
- acquire copies of the various reports

- put a fraud alert on your CRA's
- if cards were accessed or physically taken be sure to notify the bank issuing them so card authorization can be stopped and new accounts and cards can be issued.
- if cards were accessed be sure to they are processed as "account closed at consumer's request." This must be done to ensure not being held responsible for losses even though some will try to do this anyway.

You may recall I mentioned this occurring to me frequently and I had to go to court on some of them multiple times. You need to know I had notified them and they still tried to hold me accountable, so be prepared for this battle.

- If you lost checks be sure the bank is notified so they are not accepted but make sure you are not held responsible. Close the account and open new accounts, with new account numbers, cards and checks.
- Take steps to make sure fraudulent address changes have not been submitted to the U.S. Post Office or the banks or any other creditor.
- If loans have been applied for or the Social Security number has been used illegally be sure to notify the Social Security Administration.
- If you have a passport make sure to notify this office.
- Make certain no phone charges were made in your name at any address you are not aware of past or present.
- Driver's license or any other similar ID or license; be sure to notify these authorities as well.

Certegy Equifax:
This is another check service company. There are numerous such entities, and they all function similarly to that of Chex Systems and Telecheck.

International Check Service:
This is the same as Certegy but functions on an international basis.

Auto & Home Owners:

This credit reporting agency is used to track claims, payment histories and similar related data pertaining to auto and home owners policies claims in your name that have occurred in the last seven years.

Work Place Solutions:

This is a CRA that is used to track employment histories and employment related claims, acts of fraud and other work related venues. This particular CRA has not caught on as commonplace. If it does it will impede one from securing future employment should a former employer insert incorrect information. This is another CRA you will want to make certain to monitor. Currently only those with extreme blemishes tend to have files with them. The goal is to never have a file with this CRA as it will follow you and impact you long into the future.

*Note: This CRA needs to be politically excised or it will endow a select few with the ability to control the financial future of many. This will negatively impact one's future success and no one should have that power, much like no one should have the ability to take another's identity, the most valuable asset one has.

MIB (Medical Information Bureau) This CRA reports regarding insurance matters and claims experience with an individual. These include such things as policy histories relating to health insurance, auto insurance, disability insurance, long-term care insurance and numerous others.

CREDIT REPORTING AGENCIES THAT CAN HELP YOU WITH THE FIGHT AGAINST NON REPORTING ITEMS:

PRBC:

This CRA is used to report regular payments made to things not covered by the traditional bureaus. This may include such items as payday loans, insurance, utilities, land contracts payments, telephone service payments, and numerous other similar items that typically are not reported by Experian, Trans Union and Equifax or any of the other reporting agencies. This reporting agency is one you can use to aid in things that you have that report positively but do not report to other CRA's. This is accomplished through reporting this information to this firm. Up until last year you were able to report this information directly. However, now you must have a firm that grants credit or a service using CRA's as a basis for consideration. The firm can set up an account with PRBC at no cost. This will enable them to successfully provide you with the credit or service, so it is advantageous for them to aid in this credit reporting and costs them nothing to do so.

This firm is commonly used as a secondary credit reporting agency for those who lack credit or have been doing business with firms that do not report to the three primary credit bureaus. In some instances the consumer may add these items to their report or submit them to a prospective creditor looking to extend credit to them to have these items considered in the evaluation process. Several large firms, foundations, government agencies and grants fund this organization. This CRA is most commonly used in the evaluation process for major credit purchases such as a home purchase or refinance. However, this CRA is growing in popularity for those looking to establish credit who have numerous non-traditional items in good standing that do not report in the standard realms.

The establishment of this CRA can aid one in building long-term good credit and in saving money through better rates in comparison to those not having this credit worthiness proving ability.

House Of Financial Sucess

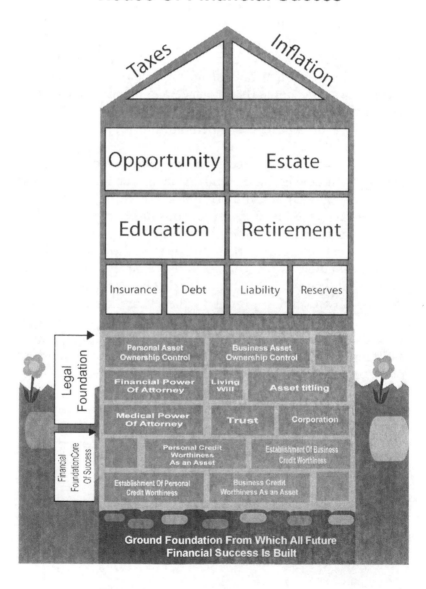

CRA'S dispute investigation requirement:

When you dispute an item with a CRA there are certain requirements per the Fair Credit Reporting Act (FCRA) that the creditor must comply with in order for the disputed items investigation to be deemed complete. The response must contain the following items without exception: name, address, person they spoke to from the creditor and corresponding telephone number of the original creditor that money is claimed to be owed to. This is in addition to the various items listed within the trade line itself that must be 100% accurate. These items might include but are not limited to balances, payment amounts, beginning and ending date, past payment history, account status and numerous other similar elements of the record. They will fail to comply because in a majority of instances information is not in their possession. In many instances they will try to secure this information from other parties. Failure of the CRA's to provide all of this information, requires that the item be removed without exception.

Chapter 7
Identity Recapture: The Working Years

Returning to my story of the identity recapture. As I stated earlier the years of 2008 and 2009 were what I would call the working years of the recapture. It was composed of working the plan that I will outline in an action plan later on. This plan of action was composed of securing a credit report, selecting no more than five items to dispute and the reasons for each item to be disputed, sending the dispute by certified mail and waiting the standard time lines depending on the type of dispute. This will be covered later in the action plan portion. Receiving the updates from the disputes and repeating the process with a creditor or the next disputed creditor as the case may be.

Secondly, during this time I had the legal service prepare letters when my personal disputes had not been successful or when a law was known to be violated. As I stated previously you would be surprised how many times the same letter on legal letterhead can have greater impact than the letter not on such letterhead. Along with these events would come those matters that had numerous prior disputes and it was now time to determine how to proceed with legal action.

This working period as I would call it is the time in which you are essentially building your case towards a creditor over time through a series of highly specific communications. The communications begin with a dispute sent by you through certified mail awaiting response. If they fail to comply disputing again for either another reason or if they are in direct violation due to not responding in proper verification format or within a specified time, then demand for the item to be removed. You may elect to engage in this process a couple of times depending on the response you receive. Whether it is a generic response, highly specific or contains falsehoods within the response itself. If these fall on deaf ears you can then contact your U.S. congressman and have him or her address the matter as a result of a violation of FCRA or the

Debt Collections Act depending on what type of creditor or information is involved. Again the disputed item in terms of type could be personal information, inquiries, or creditor trade line information (particulars relating to a creditor listing on your credit report). These particulars could be any number of variables such as the date the account was opened or closed, balance, payment history, account number, account type and so forth.

I spent all of 2008 and 2009 disputing items five at a time to each credit bureau, awaiting a response and then repeating the process for the next five. If the result was still not successful after I did this, then I would submit these compiled disputes to the legal service. They would write a legal letter to the creditor denoting their failure to comply in accordance with the FCRA or Debt Collections Practices Act as may have applied at the time. This next leads me into patterns. It is good to break things up slightly. Here is what I mean in this regard. Sometimes you dispute something and they fail to act and you immediately re-dispute the item for another reason (same creditor). While other times you use a different letter specifying that they have failed to comply. And yet other times you want to move on to another creditor and return to the creditor again and dispute again.

I mention this as sometimes depending on the particulars if you dispute the same item for the same reason or similar reason twice in a row they will simply deem it verified even though it may have not. This is a violation but occasionally they will try to get away with this due to a minor loophole and will send you what I call "staller" responses regarding these items or will deem the second complaint a mere nuisance complaint. Do not let this stand. I urge you to go through and dispute items and then if they fail to comply, send a demand for removal letter. If they claim to have updated your file, but it is still not right, re-dispute for a new reason the items that are still not right and reference the prior letter. By taking this approach you are letting it be known that they are already in violation.

This is where organization and systematization come in and I will give you the tools that I created in this regard in the resource section.

HINT:
The details, time lines, and response format are the keys to success in the recapture process. Once you have disputed a creditor numerous times or blatant violations are clearly apparent through the forming of your file on the matter in question and they have failed to comply, you are now ready to take legal action.

Again the first question is what type of creditor is involved: revolving account - installment loan - governing authority, etc.

The second question is what is the dollar amount involved?

The third question is what court are you going to file in?

Fourth, are you going to need counsel to assist you in preparation and or in representing your case (again, see prior chapter concerning counsel)

Fifth, if counsel is needed as either preparation or consult only and/or actual representation you must next select this counsel.

Sixth, now you are ready to prep your file so you are prepared to go to court. This is important and when I first started I used to do this after the case was actually filed a few days before court. I urge you not to do this. Instead, get a brown envelope with metal tongs at the flap so you can open and shut using the tines at the top. I would set up a folder for each creditor you are disputing and one for each of the CRA's. You want to create and organize your files supporting your claims, and I mean everything you have on the matter. These items would include but are not limited to the following items (keep in mind that this list is meant to merely get you stated):

- Copies of prior disputes to any credit bureau, pages relating to the creditor and the proof of certified mailing relating to the same.

- Next, any responses you have received in regards to these disputes. These include the following two pages from any credit reporting agency response, the response page and the page showing the updated listing of the creditor only. You do not need to include all of the other pages of the report that you might also receive. You need copies only, as the actual response received should be placed in the credit reporting agency folder as received in chronological order. You do this for two reasons: one, so you know where to find it if you need it in the future and two, the copy is placed in the creditor folder so you are ready for court.

- Any legal letter sent in your behalf by counsel or the U.S congressman or any other regulator you may have contacted in relation to the creditor involved. These are the many industry regulators I mentioned in chapter one.

- You want to make a bullet point list of the violations and be specific with amounts, dates etc., as you will use this when you present your case.

You will also want to include any filings you may have also made such as police reports or agency regulator complaints with any exhibit copies that you submitted with complaints and proof of delivery.

GROUP THOSE ITEMS INTO PILES BY CATEGORY AND PLACE EACH CATEGORY IN CHRONOLOGICAL ORDER AND THEN ORGANIZE THE ITEMS IN ORDER OF PRIORITY.

Lastly, keep a running list of all items enclosed in the packet. You want to do this so that in case you pull something out to copy it, you can make sure it is put back in its place. You are now ready to file the court case and have the court notice served on the other party. You want to make sure you get a receipt for all expenses. When you get back home copy these receipts and do the following with them:

Place the originals behind your summary list of items enclosed.

Next you want to place a consolidated photocopy of these expenses in the back of the folder and use them in court, not the originals. You want to do this in case the judge requires a copy to be submitted to the court and you can then retain the originals. Never give the originals.

Lastly, take a second photocopy of these receipts and place it in a separate brown envelope labeled "summary expenses." You might ask why would you want to do this. It will enable you to have your expenses in a single envelope in chronological order and will make it so you do not have to pull out all of the individual folders if the only questions is past cost. In the very front, again I would have a sheet with spaces for entry. The entry would include the creditor, type of expense, cost and the total expenses on a running basis. I have a sample sheet in the reference section for you to use.

Behind this I would include a page for each creditor so you can have a running total for each individual creditor. That way, the day before court you can make sure that you have all the original receipts in your creditor folder and copies in the expense folder. Pay these expenses out of the separate checking account. This will enable you if needed to be able to provide a copy of the cancelled check or bank statement to serve as proof of payment in addition to the expense item's receipt. By having a separate checking account you avoid having to divulge unrelated personal items in passing, as the account is designed solely for identity theft recapture related items.

I spent 2008 and 2009 repeating this process with each CRA, disputing five items per bureau. Wait no longer than 30 days for a response, and then move on to the next round of disputes. Secondly you can also dispute items that are blatantly wrong

with the creditors directly. However, I have found it is best
to initially dispute through the CRA rather than the creditor
directly, at least initially.

If you systematized as I outlined in the resource section you
will spend a couple of hours a week at most handling things as
responses come in.

HINT:
Be sure to provide proof of identity (copy of social security
card and driver's license, black & white only) with all
submissions or they will be stalled or ignored altogether, no
exceptions. Even if your counsel sends the letter. Additionally,
some creditors will demand a notarized affidavit to speak to
your attorney. This is a stall tactic in most cases but not all so
have an affidavit prepared that is generic and make copies of
this as well. It will most commonly be used later in the process,
not initial disputes unless filing an insurance or similar claim.

The second phase of actions was the filing of the disputes with
the various regulators. This can take time and each agency
will have its own processes and you have to comply with this
fully as well. There is the filing and going to court on the
various matters once a matter's file has been built through the
dispute process outlined thus far. When I started this process
I had more than thirty-seven pages of fraud on each of my
credit reports and different creditors from bureau to bureau.
Seeing as I was disputing only five at a time it takes time to
simply go through the process and patience is required as they
will set roadblocks along the way. I urge you to be careful
when responding to requests for additional items, as they are
sometimes actually trying to trip you up. Again, the bureaus
are on the creditor's side, not yours, and it is critical that you
understand this.

HINT:
Only answer relevant questions asked, but respond to all
requests regardless.

This is the grueling stage of the process as I began to dispute items and then move onto the next and then revisit those needing second disputes or an actual violation. This is when court filing and packets needing to be prepared for those matters requiring an attorney for suit were required to be prepared in an effort to prepare the attorney. This is the second reason it is important to make the creditor file early on and simply add things to it as you go. Because if you at some stage need to hire an attorney you can simply take the envelope to a copy center and copy them quickly and send to counsel.

I also took the items in the folders and scanned them into my computer and created a folder by creditor name and within this electronic record I broke the matter into two groups, support items and correspondence with the attorney and from the attorney. By taking this approach if an attorney needed a single item you can go to your e-mail and simply attach the item and send it to him or her quickly. I was also making it a practice when I sent items whether by mail or e-mail to send a follow-up e-mail and recap conversation request confirmation of receipt of said items. I then created a list in my e-mail account by attorney and a sub folder by creditor. By taking this approach I was able to maintain an electronic record of my communications with the attorney.

This is important in case you need them for reference purposes with the attorney in the future. Moreover, if you have to replace the attorney and need to bring the new counsel up to speed this is an effective way to let them know what has transpired. Early on when I was fine tuning my short list of attorneys it was occasionally needed to make an attorney change. This was for many reasons, sometimes the attorney was good but simply too busy and could not make the matter a priority. This cannot be allowed, as some items have critical deadlines that must be followed to the letter. In the resource section I will provide you with tracking sheets for all of this. Other times they were simply the wrong attorney for the type of law or the creditor involved. You have to think of this as hiring a temporary employee and making sure you have the right person for the job, as success is required. Having the wrong person for the job is worse than detrimental to this objective.

I took the electronic records matter a step further and as each credit report update came in I scanned each page individually, not as a single document. This was done so that if an attorney needed a specific page or you had to send an exhibit or supporting document to a creditor this could be done effectively and made future reference simple. I created a folder for each CRA on my computer and as the reports came in I created sub folders for each response by date. At the end of the year I created a sub folder named that CRA and year and moved the sub folders above folders into it. This makes future reference simple, creditor first and then by year and then by respective response. This organization as you begin to get multiple responses coming in from creditors, CRA's, regulators, courts, etc., makes keeping things organized simple. Finally, I put all of the folders in a box and start a new box every year; even if a matter is still open at year-end start a new folder and put it in the new year's box.

Now that I have outlined what I spent my time doing during this grueling and monotonous period you need to be aware of some of the reactions that were also being taken. It was at this stage that an additional level of frustration began to set in as many government agencies that were supposed to be helping me sometimes were letting the creditor off the hook. As I have stated numerous times they are looking out for the industry members, not your interests. This sometimes meant I had to file appeals or go to regulators above them to get matters handled. Additionally, sometimes items you have removed will reappear and you have to address this very strongly with formal specific disputes as these creditors will commonly remove something and then try to reinsert the item. This is where constantly monitoring your credit will enable this to be seen when it happens. Once you get everything cleaned up you will still want to check this consistently to make certain that all of the contents of the report are correct.

This is also the stage when I was unable to get all of the regulators to act properly and had to go to their regulators. This is where generally you will contact such parties as your U.S. congressman, state senator, U.S. senator, governor, etc. This is also when I learned that if the creditor involved resides in another state sometimes you have to contact the regulators in the state where the company resides or has their corporate office. I have had mixed experiences in this regard, some good and some bad. Sometimes you have to file the complaint in the company's home state and they will then forward it to the regulator's office in the state where you reside. This is good in many cases as it elevates its priority, as it then falls under interstate commerce and additional laws can be present to aid you in protections. However, also understand that this sometimes can also add bureaucracy to the situation but is important to be gone through to build your case in the event that you are later forced to take the matter to court. Also realize that even if a regulator denies your request for assistance, it does not necessarily mean you do not have a claim. It is simply a claim outside their scope so do not take this to mean that a regulator saying they will not help you does not mean you do not have a course of action at your disposal. Again this is not legal advice but merely my experience.

Be prepared for political retribution as I call it, as sometimes if you have to go over a person's or agency's head they will try to make your life difficult so be prepared for this to occur. I realize it is difficult to understand if you were a victim of identity theft why they would do this, but they will because the companies pay their lobbying groups for this privilege of preferential treatment.

Once you have gone through this process with a number of creditors a couple of things will eventually emerge. One is your confidence in your ability to handle situations. Secondly, you will begin to see patterns with certain creditors, creditor types, specific regulators and so on. However, as you press on and these parties noted above see you are not going away, they will do one of two things. They will either try to shut you down every time you submit a subsequent request and pass it off as nuisance in nature or they will see that you have truly been a victim and will begin to help you solve the problem. Sometimes they will still only help on a limited basis, but others will then begin to go out of their way to help you to right the wrong. This will vary from person to person, agency to agency and state to state so all you can do is work the system within the law's parameters. This is when you will start to see a thaw in the icy wall of blockage. It is at this stage that you begin to gain credibility and subsequent claims are given more weight. This will not happen overnight and will typically occur in the last 1/3 of your battle. But I'm pointing it out to let you know that when you start to see this you are in the last third of the process, and it is yet another milestone in the process.

This is also when you will begin to go to court more frequently on the earlier built files and win. When the first third of matters disputed early on begin to go to court is when you are entering the third segment of the initial responses so you can use this as a guide as to how long it will take you to complete the process. The actual timeline will greatly vary from person to person based on the types of creditors involved, the size of the creditors, the number of creditors involved and other similar particulars to your situation. I had 37 pages so I knew when I was dealing with the last third of the 37 pages that I was getting close. I am not completely finished with this stage as of the writing of this book; however, the end is in sight.

It is also at this stage that I urge you to begin to build new credit and rebuild your credit record while you complete the cleanup, whether you need credit or not. A wise mentor told me back when I was in college to build credit when you do not need it so it is there when you do. If you wait until you do it will be too late, as no one will lend you money when you need it -- only when you do not. The principle is simple: make it always look like you do not need it but will use it to build a relationship if offered. This mindset will be critical to your long-term financial success.

TO DO LIST: Build credit when you do not need it so you have when you do need it.

HINT:
Manage your credit profile in terms the types of creditors shown, number of creditors shown, age of accounts shown, etc.

*Note: Having the right mix will allow you to maximize your score. There are firms that can aid you with this. One example of this is credit optimization firms (see www.planningwithmerit.com members only area for quality optimization firm). This is in no way touting them but rather so you can use them to perform a Google search (enter "credit optimization firm") and find others that service your area. Again, I do not promote any specific vendors but merely give examples of those that have served me well.

- One of the leading reasons for this is that the CEO of this company was the founder of one of the firms I hired early on who was subsequently fired in a related industry. Situations like this are why I do not promote any companies but rather take the approach of telling you the type of professionals you need and how to evaluate them and leave the selection process to you. I have also found that certain firms are sometimes more effective in certain regions, and this avoids me promoting a firm that is not effective in your region. One might ask why I did not name this firm specifically as when you Google search this firm you will see a number of other search words and their competition also appear. Although I have heard good things about this firm I have chosen to use a firm that was more effective in my region initially, but subsequently hired the firm in question and received excellent service in spite of the prior bad experience with the parties sister firm. Decisions like these need to be made by the reader as you based on the facts available

The key point is to start the rebuilding process as early in the process as possible. However, I found that until you get the majority of the derogatory items off this could be rather difficult.

Good Foundation

Personal Asset Ownership Control	Business Asset Ownership Control	
Financial Power Of Attorney	Living Will	Asset titling
Medical Power Of Attorney	Trust	Corporation

Legal Foundation

Personal Credit Worthiness As an Asset	Establishment Of Business Credit Worthiness
Establishment Of Personal Credit Worthiness	Business Credit Worthiness As an Asset

Financial Foundation-Core Of Success

Ground Foundation From Which All Future Financial Success Is Built

Vs.

Bad Foundation

No Legal Foundation

No Powers Of Attorney

No Corporation

No Will

Lack Of Personal Credit

Lack Of Business Credit Worthiness

Lack Of Legal Foundation

No Financial Foundation Core Of Success

Foundation Built On Quick Sand

DO NOT: wait to start this process
DO NOT: take government official's word as the law of the land
DO NOT: deviate from the process of disputes or rebuilding, as it will only cause greater delay, greater damage and larger costs to get back on track.

I learned this the hard way so learn from my mistakes and learning curve. This is one of the primary things you must take from this book, to learn from my mistakes and do not repeat them or make mistakes of your own. If you follow the path outlined in the resource directory and this narrative story of my battle you will avoid the unneeded and unwarranted detours and expenses that go with them.

The working years will also let you know how trustworthy your vendors, government officials and other parties involved in your battle are. Sometimes the strangest things will happen in your favor and at other times things will appear against you out of nowhere.

This is your government at work so embrace it. However, I found before I could face it I had to fix it. You see, while I was waging my battle for identity recapture I found a judge and a couple of government agency officials were out to get me and I realize how this must sound. Yet it was later determined that even before the identity theft these parties were engaged in an act to damage me and the identity theft event simply allowed them to capitalize on my misfortune. I would be the first to admit this sounds like paranoia. Which is why I dismissed the notion for several years. However, in 2006 the evidence appeared and I dismissed it. It reappeared briefly in 2007 and I dealt with it briefly but not fully.

However, in 2008 and 2009 the matter reappeared once again and I had to deal with it firmly. I began waging this battle and in 2010, as of the date of this book being written the matter is on the calendar to be solved once and for all. I anticipate this not being fully solved until sometime into mid to late 2014 as the battle is currently awaiting appeal in federal court and is expected to be heard sometime in 2014 after enduring countless delays and stall tactics from the parties involved. Again I want to stress that you must take these battles as they come and deal with them strongly and firmly without reservation. This will minimize the need to deal with them repeatedly. I urge you to learn from my mistakes. When an event occurs that is intentionally causing you harm, take decisive action. Make sure you hit the other side so hard they do not get up and that it is a knockout punch and widely known, as this will deter others from taking similar action. You need to instill absolute fear when possible. The other side not knowing how extreme of an action you are willing to take is the best offense. When I walk into a room and these enemies are present I want my mere presence to make them uncomfortable. In addition to taking this matter to federal court and the pending appeal, I filed complaints with related regulators and prepared a press release and sent it to the editorial departments of multiple newspapers, TV, and radio stations locally, regionally and nationally. You want to take this action as it prevents the regulators from sweeping it under the rug and also prevents the truth from being polluted with lies from the other side. However, this will open you up to scrutiny so be prepared to back-up what you say, rather than to slander the other side even if it is warranted (and there will be instances that it will be). Again, that's where building your respective files will come in handy yet once again for reference and to give anyone that needs proof that what you say is true. Remember when you are the identity theft victim it is you that has to prove that the facts exist. You may recall when I started the book and stated that many times you will be the one with the burden of proof. This is merely yet another example but it sets the stage to minimize the need to prove your point in the future. As once it becomes widely known and you have proven your claims to be fact multiple times, it becomes easier and eventually you are believed and people begin to aid you but it is not a short process. Returning to my story of the judge...

You see, a judge was working with the agency in question to wage war and damage my efforts by inserting falsehoods in my background. This was an attempt to paint a tainted image on my tragedy and further exacerbate it by causing me financial damage through creating even more injustice. While I am being cryptic in this I have to be to a degree as a number of legal matters are pending. These legal matters are very serious and thus I must be cryptic in nature. However, the short of it is we found that through third-party verification the two parties noted above were engaged in willful blindness, malicious and tortuous conduct and other similar claims. This has forced me to seek damages and file suit civilly and the officials may not only face financial damages, but could also face loss of job and even criminal charges. I will be the first to admit it was never my intent to be the maverick crusader in matters of this type. However, sometimes you are forced to take this role whether you want to or not. This was required not only to be repaid for the damages I endured but to ensure it does not happen to others.

When I began this battle it soon and early on became known that the regulators had received several other similar complaints but had dismissed them. I cannot stress enough that these regulators will a lot of times not do their job until they are forced to do so. When others that previously filed claims found out of my much more serious series of claims they began contacting me. We then all contacted the regulators individually at once. This made it abundantly clear that the injured parties were not going away. This matter has subsequently been forwarded to the State of Michigan's administrative Supreme Court, the chief justice and other similar officials that were being kept in the dark by the lower level regulators. But these parties did nothing, so the matter was moved to federal court and will be heard in 2014

As of the writing of this book, through my actions noted above, i.e., of going on the offensive, the supervising judge that was acting with misconduct has resigned his position, and several state agency personnel also involved have lost their supervisory position and or have been replaced, though not all. This exposure has caused several other judges in the building in unrelated matters to also be investigated and one judge is now electing to retire after enduring an investigation by the Judicial Tenure Commission. Furthermore, yet a third investigation is just beginning, at my insistence, on another matter involving myself and a third judge, all within the same district court.

It was never my intent to be the crusader as I stated before. However, sometimes you simply have to step up and right the wrong even if it does not benefit you directly. My repeated exposures of misconduct caused the other parties' complaints to be taken with greater gravity. For example, a woman's case was deemed sexual harassment in the workplace and resulted in not only a civil settlement but the Judicial Tenure Commission coming in and encouraging the judge to retire. In my opinion he should be behind bars. However, as I have said numerous times before in this book, these supposed consumer protection agencies are there for those they oversee, not the consumer as they actually claim.

Additionally, due to the fact that the matter involved judges, attorneys and referees the judicial tenure commission was also brought into the equation.

This will be heard in federal appeals court in late 2014 as noted above.

It is for this reason after countless delays that in early 2013 all of the matters involving the county officials and remaining judge matters have been moved into federal court and are expected to make their way to appeals court also in mid to late 2014.

Similarly, if the remaining items in state court have the same fate these matters will also be moved to federal court for legal action.

I feel it is imperative that you realize you will not always know where a battle may take you. However, the road in any case will be bumpy but you must take the journey nonetheless.

Many times you will be made whole monetarily and paid for the harm you were caused and sometime the money will make things better but realize not all wounds can be healed with money, though it can go a long way to starting the healing process. As I said, when I began this battle in 2006 I was in no way even remotely expecting the events to unfold as they have up until this point in the process. I can tell you I am glad I took the challenge not only because I have begun to regain my good name and established a firm foundation for future success. I have lost a great deal of time that could have gone into my long-term success. However, sometimes you have to take a large step back to make giant leaps forward in your long-term success and recognizing these times are why following a road map to success in any endeavor is so critical. Being the trail-blazer is an experience of ongoing trauma. This trauma is endured so others do not have to endure it in the future. That is the purpose of this book.

However, such events ultimately make one stronger and much more able to see these success springboards in the road ahead and aids one in sidestepping financial and professional land mines also in the path you are headed. If you look at anyone who is successful they have had mentors. These mentors change from time to time and endeavor to endeavor. I learned this while I was in college while starting my first business. This opportunity exposed me to very successful people in many areas of specialty and the common theme was told to me like this. Pick a path you want to pursue and then find someone who has been extremely successful in that path and emulate them by extracting out the right things to do. However, realize these people like all others have made mistakes and make sure to recognize these as well so you do not repeat their mistakes. The identity recapture process is like any other successful endeavor; you are only as strong as your weakest link. With this in mind it is critical you monitor those around you in terms of vendors, advisors, friends and family. You will be surprised how many times I have seen family members sabotage other people's success. Vendors are the same way, because the sooner they fix your problem 100% the sooner they will be removed from the team. This becomes a matter of managing those around you in all capacities. As I stated earlier in this book the process will make you jaded at times so you have to manage this point as well.

Continuing on with the government agencies and regulators, I will discuss in the next chapter Consumers Energy and the role they played and continue to play. Additionally, I will expound on another government event similar to the court event outlined above relating to the identity theft. I am asked many times when people read the next chapter if I felt victimized, singled out and mad. The answer is yes but you have to use this to focus your energy on getting even. This may sound confrontational and it is. As you will see in the next chapter the parties involved will revisit some of our past players. The matter of identity recapture has to be viewed like a war and up until now all you have heard is a series of battles in that war. As you have heard thus far, I have won some, lost some and some were a draw, but they all have to be fought. The only way you truly lose is to give up the fight. I also want to stress at this point that for the average person their identity theft in most cases (though not all) will be nowhere near as ruthless as mine has been. I have also found that the damage is typically in direct proportion to that of the person involved. What I mean here is those who use credit more or have different roles in society in terms of everyday activities are more susceptible to the wrath like that I have experienced. In short, the more you are seen by the public the bigger target you make. However, that simply makes it more important that the battle be waged, both diligently and successfully.

Chapter 8
Monopoly Industries and Identity Theft War

When you are battling identity theft you will find that many companies you have dealt with for years and those you have no choice in dealing with will cause you problems. This leads me into the next portion of my story, which deals with the monopolies we all interact with on a daily basis and think nothing about it. Many firms fall into this category. The one I had this problem with was Consumers Energy. While Consumers Energy may not be the provider in your area they are the provider in mine and there is by far no more corrupt an organization. You see, like in most areas there is typically only one utility provider for such items as gas, electric, water and similar services. Because they are the only game in town you are forced to play by their rules. This would not be a problem if we all knew what the rules were. Of course, we don't. Worse yet they are always changing and you do not even know it. You need to understand that the carrier makes all the rules. While the government oversees their activities it is not really to enforce the rules. Utilities are by far the worst of the monopolies in this country.

If there is a rules change that is unfavorable to the utility they simply add an additional fee to your bill. If this is not bad enough they are commonly known for continuous and ongoing fraud that is so frequent it has become commonplace. You will be amazed when you hear my story and how I became aware of all this. Once I outline it and the impact it had on my identity theft you may even become scared. Please understand the purpose of this book is to educate so you can deal with your identity theft and it is not intended to serve as a political agenda of any kind. Though I like anyone else have an opinion, this forum is not intended to express it but to expose the injustice relating to Consumers Energy as related to identity theft recapture.

When you are an identity theft victim as I have been this is by far one of the first vendors you will want to contact to make certain other addresses have not had utility accounts opened in your name. If this has occurred, get on it and go directly to the regulator and make it known. They will more than likely dismiss you and claim you are simply trying to get out of an owed bill so be prepared; it happened to me. First, the regulator that oversees utilities in most states is the public service commission. The group first of all is not a traditional regulator as they pass themselves off as a mediator. However, the reality is they have a grievance process, their own court system using an administrative judge, and little to no appeal process. The deck is stacked against you as they work with the utility every day, so know that they are not going to work too hard in your interest because they will have to deal with the utility tomorrow also.

My story here begins long before the actual identity theft. I feel it is important you understand this history, as it will play a huge role in the investigation following the identity theft. It goes back to 2003 when I had an apartment at an apartment complex. I chose not to renew my lease but the apartment complex claimed I did even though they were never able to put forth a signed renewed lease. At the time I moved out at the end of my lease, paid my final utility bill and took the utilities out of my name. The apartment complex moved a new tenant into the unit but rather than the utilities going into the new tenant's name they were placed back in mine. You might say well this is an easy fix -- and you would not be farther from the truth. The apartment complex tried to take me to court to say that I renewed my lease and failed to pay and left a balance with the utility company, which simply was not true. I filed what is called an informal complaint with the public service commission and when the investigation was all done they ended up forcing me to settle a fraction of the original bill totaling more than $350 when I used none of the services. Problem solved? Wrong. You see, for the remainder they issue a utility credit and apply it to your current bill wherever you reside now. If you do not have utilities in your name they make every attempt to get out of paying it in cash. If you do have service, what they will do is issue a credit for the amount of the credit. Again, problem solved? Wrong again. They then do the following: crank up your utility bill to eat the credit away. You might ask, how do they do this? It is a simple answer. They go with estimate billing rather than actual billing.

So I went to the public service commission again and filed another complaint. This time I started again with the informal complaint but given the animosity I was forced to file a formal complaint eventually. I was to be issued a credit of $274 dollars. OK, problem solved... wrong. They then wait for you to get utilities in your name again and then require you have a security deposit to get utilities in your name by claiming you have unsettled prior balances. It's not true but remember these regulators work with the utility every day and are not working for you as they claim. This time I assigned the matter to my legal service and after numerous legal letters back and forth I was once again forced to settle a balance which essentially was the balance claimed several years prior that had been previously settled. This essentially voids out the prior settlement. I had refused to pay so they refused to allow utilities to not only be put in my name but also in a home that I am known to live in. Remember these people control the game. You might be thinking, well simply put the utilities in your relative or friend's name. No dice. They look at who is on title and hold any grievances with these names against the property in terms of its ability to gain access to utilities.

You might say this is morally wrong and you would be right, but you do not know half the story yet. In Michigan, as in many other states you are eligible for home heating credits to reimburse you for a portion of your utility costs for the prior year when you file your tax return. To qualify for this credit you typically have to make under a certain dollar amount of annual income or have numerous variables to comply such as number of family members and square footage of home and so on. When the state issues this credit the utility company takes control of these proceeds through a voucher that is either sent to the utility company directly and applied to your account as a credit or a check with both your name and the utility's name on it. When you receive it you sign it and mail it to your utility provider and they again issue a credit to your bill. However, your bill will typically be the amount of the credit or substantially higher than usual when applied in an effort to diminish the impact it has on your bill. This is intentional. In my case I learned that a number of my vouchers had been received, cashed and applied and my bills in these months were sometimes as much as five times the actual bill. How is this possible? The answer is again estimated billing. You spend the next several months fighting with the firm over your bill and they issue some credits but in the end they have cheated you. This is wrong! And you do not even know the half of it.

Remember I have now settled the bill on numerous prior occasions and it has now essentially been paid in full more than twice. They take this old account and reinsert the entire bill on your current bill and if you refuse to pay they threaten to shut your utilities off until paid. They then turn the matter over to collections and place the matter on your credit report even though it was previously settled in full multiple times already. You say, that's wrong... well, I have not told you the whole story yet. You see, even if you have not had these experiences the utility many times will openly admit (as employees have to me) that when they have someone who does not pay their bills, they simply divide the unpaid balance up among people who do pay their bills. They will pay it or the utility will shut their services off.

Let me tell you, this is not rare occurrence, but the norm. You might say, "Well clearly if the officials knew this they would correct it," but I am here to tell you that you are flat-out wrong. They knew it and have they always known it. You see, this surplus of cash is one of the many places they get their funds to influence officials with PAC (Political Action Committee) contributions. This is not the sole source but a large one nonetheless.

I have had officials threaten me with violence, put me on lists and months later reinserted false bills, as well as fail to make payments and adjustments. The purpose is to keep the bill in utter flux so that you have trouble realizing the actual cost so it becomes harder and harder to know what the true bill is. I have now gone in front of the public service committee three times and won three times. However, they are hollow victories as all they do is issue a credit and the process starts all over again and once you are on the list you will have problems with Consumers the rest of your life.

Now that I have given you the history let me bring you up to date following the identity theft. You may remember I lost the house to foreclosure with the home being in redemption through August 2008 with the redemption beginning February of that year. Now what if I told you I requested following Thanksgiving of 2007 for all utilities to be turned off but that this did not occur until December 27, 2007. What if I further told you they continued to bill me for services that were never rendered including a required deposit through the end of the redemption period in August of 2008 and that these bills were not only based on fraud but estimated bills. What if I told you I was present when the services were physically turned off and had a witness. You would say I have a pretty strong case for fraud, right? Well, the public service commission did not agree and refused to allow me to get service until the fraudulent bill was paid in full. This matter was scheduled to go to federal court in late 2010 and in addition to the actual damages civil damages are being sought in this matter.

The case of Consumers Energy finally began in 2010 and the attorney representing me tried to pull a fast one and I was forced to file a complaint with the Michigan Bar relating to the attorney. Once this happened not a single attorney in the state would take the case. I ended up representing myself in district court. The defendant's legal team made several attempts to dismiss and stall the case. However, once Consumers Energy's legal team realized I was going to bring forth a pattern of misconduct and had put together a list of people to be parties to the suit and that the matter would turn into a class action suit, they mysteriously "found" the records. They were able to interpret them correctly and the fraudulent bill evaporated overnight. . You would say finally solved... and you would once again be wrong. You see, one of the claims that Consumers Energy then made was that several of the respective years' home heating credits were either not applied for or not actually received by them. This forced me to take on the Michigan treasury.

By this point I had been through many battles and the file that I was built was thick. I was able to prove not only that I had applied and received these home heating credits, but that Consumers Energy did too. Then it was claimed that the credits had been applied to someone else's account in error. One would surely then think that this can easily be corrected. Wrong. In the end I was forced to sue the Michigan treasury for each respective year's home heating credit in dispute and this involved seven years in all. As of the writing of this book in 2013 there are still disputes relating to this matter being handled legally in both Michigan treasury and IRS terms. As you will learn later they tried to play hot potato bouncing the home heating credit refunds between agencies first claiming I owed the Michigan treasury taxes. When this was disproved they then claimed I owed the IRS and tried to send it to them. When this was disproved they then tried to send it to a series of state agencies at the behest of my favorite judge and state agency nemesis team. When this was disproved it was then sent back to the Michigan treasury. This case is expected to be heard in late 2013, early 2014 due to the current political turmoil and the current federal and some state agencies being shut-down due to the congressional dispute with the president.

I have not even mentioned the fact that while the dispute was underway with Consumers Energy originally in 2008, that when I visited their local office they claimed threats were made which were not. The police were called and the police sided with me. However, I was later forced to deal with this false claim and filed actions on Consumers Energy and as a result

I am not permitted on their property and when they visit my property the police have to be present without exception. This involved me filing a police report and charges of my own. The matter was never heard by a judge due to the clout of Consumers Energy, which leads me back to the lobbyists and the previous examples of politics overriding the law of the land. This is a corrupt process and needs to be corrected.

Up until this point I have always said to file in the court that makes the most economic sense. This is the only exception to that rule and here is why. The utility is state funded so you want to file this in federal court to avoid the good ole boy network from ruling against you even though your case is rock solid. This matter has been reported on many news channels over the years yet none of the officials solve the problem. However, federal court is very formal and they will litigate each claim and award damages accordingly. You want this matter filed in federal court and if you know you are going to go to court on this, it is the only exception that you will not only want to file in federal court but also will want legal counsel as they will always be represented. This organization is the poster child of the legal mafia and they intend to grind on you until you give. Federal courts will award damages for their actions and these awards will generally give you the funds to deal with the injustices that will follow. The only way to avoid the retribution is to move to an area not covered by that utility which is most commonly another state. You can expect this to be one of the first matters that you start with and one of the last matters to solve. It is the only matter of its kind you will deal with and a prime example of why monopolies of its kind promote corruption and injustice and willful blindness by those who oversee them. As I state in this book the laws are there to protect you but it is up to you to cause them to be enforced. The pendulum in this regard is beginning to shift in favor of the consumers but we are not yet there. Half the battle is knowing what to do.

You must also realize that these monopolies network with other monopolies in related industries. Some examples of this include the local cable company or phone company; firms like Charter communications and AT & T are known for similar forms of corruption and malfeasance. It is not uncommon for one vendor to let the others know if they have a difficult client in their eyes with events like those I expressed above. If this is passed along they many times will try to partake in similar acts of abuse. If you can prove that the other party informed them you can sue them severely for privacy breaches and similar claims but consult legal counsel as I am not a lawyer. One similar vendor I was forced to escort them off my property with the assistance of police. They will make all kinds of claims about entering your property -- do not let them slide. I became aware of all of this due to my identity theft and others trying to order such services in my name at other locations. As you have heard me say multiple times throughout this book I do not promote vendors but I do promote who not to use. One vendor tried to make violence claims against me when I had witnesses to the contrary. Think of the most unscrupulous person you can think of and put them in a truck and you have just painted the picture of the typical employee they hire and literally pay a fee for services rendered. They further try to shield themselves by passing them off as independent contractors but do not fall for this line either. They can still be held liable for their actions as you did not hire the individual you hired a firm and they chose to sub contract. In short your contract is with them not the sub-contractor so do not be fooled by these tactics.

Firms that fall into this realm of monopolies all function the same way. While you may not have experienced this malfeasance yet it is simply a matter of time. I guarantee that if you asked 10 people at least a third of them would have a bad experience of some kind to tell. The key here is when you are a victim of identity theft you are largely more exposed to corruption of this type. You may recall earlier in this book I stated that once you have been a victim of identity theft you would be exposed to more scoundrels than before the identity theft. What most people do not realize is they have always been dealing with the scoundrels but now they are exposed. Once you are a victim of identity theft you are amongst the people these scoundrels attack because your credibility is damaged and they use this to their advantage. But do not take it, you have to aggressively defend yourself. Monopolies are probably one of the most important battles you must wage, otherwise they will follow you forever. Unlike a credit report, where, though it may take years, items will eventually go away, a utility service is something that can make your life miserable forever, unless you move. Even then they still may cause problems as many times when you move to a new city they will check with the prior utility to confirm you are credit worthy. This is one of the most important battles of them all because we all need utilities to function every day and this demand is what gives them the power and you must take control of the situation without exception.

Upon completion of the federal battle I am preparing criminal charges against the parties involved as a number of high level Consumers Energy executives knew of my plight and enhanced its wrath intentionally. This is misconduct that falls into the criminal realm. You may not be required to take things to this level. One of the reasons so many asked me to write this book was because I was the poster child for extreme identity theft as far as cases go. You see, many times when others are a victim of identity theft a few accounts are opened, accessed and they are able to solve it quickly. My case is by far the exception to the rule, though cases like mine are becoming far more commonplace than even a few years ago when my problem began. Since my battle began the numbers on an annual basis have doubled several times over. This problem is growing at epidemic proportions and you cannot wait for the government to step in and help, as more than likely it will not happen and if it does it will be too late for so many. The tools are already there for protection. The key is to know what they are and where they are so you can access them.

Chapter 9
The Status of the Story

As of the writing of this book we are now in late 2013 Given the impending battles I have left to wage before my identity recapture is complete I anticipate being fully complete sometime in 2015 if all goes well. Again, let me stress that if you follow some of the guidelines I will outline in the next chapter regarding identity protection, the systems outlined in the resources section and use those items effectively and consistently the battle for the average person will be much shorter than mine. Additionally, avoiding many of the mistakes I made along the way will greatly shorten your timeline. When it is all said and done this experience was an education that I wish I had not had to endure. Nonetheless, I am a stronger person because of it and many of the techniques have already proven helpful within my business in terms of dealing with creditors since the identity theft tragedy.

It is anticipated that the creditor suits in federal court will be complete sometime in the summer of 2014 and then only the class action lawsuits that have developed out of these challenges will remain until sometime in 2015. If all continues on schedule, the civil suits will follow shortly after that, again if all remains on schedule. However, one thing that I can say with the utmost certainty is that there will always be challenges and I suspect there will be others between now and the end of this battle.

One attorney I worked with early on said it best and I hope you take this point with you. While it comes off as sarcastic there is nothing closer to the truth: "once you are a victim of identity theft and have even cleaned up the fraud, you will spend the rest of your life protecting your identity from further fraud." It is proven that those exposed to identity theft once are far more likely to have it happen again. This may sound defeatist but knowing this fact is half the battle. Following the steps I have outlined in the next chapter will greatly diminish the likelihood of a second theft but there are no guarantees in life except for death and taxes. This book was written as the first in a series of books to help the layman reach his goals. There are many books out there to help one reach their goals, tell someone's story, etc. The list goes on and on. You name it and there is a book on it. The purpose of this book is to aid people in building financial protection of their identity and the subsequent books will be written to aid people in building his/ her financial house of success. What success means to each individual is different so I will leave that interpretation to you for contemplation. This book is merely the ground upon which one's financial house is built. Unlike many of the other books out there, I have combined four valuable experiences together in this one book. It contains the how to, the "what not to do" and examples of events that will occur if you ignore the first two. Lastly, I give you examples and structure from which to build your own success if the tragedy of identity theft strikes you.

The next chapter is meant to serve as steps that can be taken as acts of prevention of identity theft, or, if it has already happened, to prevent it from happening again in the future. The last half of this book is the resource section. I have broken the resource section into a series of mini sections to make it an easy reference. You will see similar sections that have been mentioned in the story portion, but please realize this is not simply a restatement of these points but additional points in this realm; though some will be restated others will be material that was not previously mentioned. This is the case with many sections within the resource section such as hints, to do's and not to do's. The story only exposed those aspects of identity theft that applied to my situation, but every person's experiences with identity theft will be unique and it is critical to understand this. I would like to say my story with identity theft is the worst, but there are by far worse out there. Mine, however, is generally deemed more severe than the majority of known cases. As I told you this battle would be waged on many fronts from financial, emotional and numerous others.

The key is to keep plugging along through the battle. If you
stop fighting, you will lose. I have seen people take this
approach and saw the slow, agonizing demise of their life as
they knew it. The key is to stay focused. Once success in the
battle of identity theft recapture begins to be achieved you
will grow in confidence, but it is a process and not a process
that is amenable to shortcuts. However, there is a path of least
resistance and that is the purpose of this book: to make that
path available through the use of a workable action plan that
can be adapted to your specific situation.

Chapter 10
Identity Theft Preventative Measures

Identity theft prevention is not like when one is robbed at knife or gunpoint and can prevent it by simply not going to a particular part of town. Identity theft is like being robbed when you are away from home. You see, most thefts occur through sources that you do business with every day. Either their place of business is robbed as in my case, a bad employee acts improperly or a hacker breaches the office through the computer. This does not mean, though, that there are not measures that can be taken to prevent identity theft. This injustice can come in many forms and protecting yourself as much as possible is the most you can do in terms of prevention.

There are a few things that one can do to prevent identity theft that are broad in spectrum but very effective. First, you should photocopy every item in your wallet from the photos, credit cards front and back, membership cards... everything. Then put them in the order they appear in your wallet, staple the photocopies and place them in a strong box or safe. Secondly, do not use names or passwords that can be easily guessed by others. Change your passwords at least twice per year on a non-scheduled basis. Third, every time you speak to a vendor you do business with, write down the time, date, name and the purpose or outcome of the call. If an identity theft occurs later on this will enable you to reference these prior conversations effectively. In these notes be sure to express any animosity or reluctance of the person to perform any task or requests.

If you shop or use the Internet be sure to have a strong firewall and only access sites that are safe with strong firewall and industry standards as a minimum in terms of encryption of technology. Only access accounts of a financial nature from personal computers. Avoid accessing such information from public domains, libraries or other public sources as the information can be retained on these servers and give unintended parties access to this information.

When you go to a business institution such as a bank or similar provider keep account numbers and similar items out of sight while waiting in line, as others in line will look over your shoulder to gain this information. When planning to visit such a business have items such as deposits and withdrawal slips prepared in advance rather than at the counter. Avoid stating account numbers, social security numbers and similar things of this nature out loud as this ensures that others cannot gain this information.

Next is a common one that most banks in particular ignore. When you complete a transaction do not throw the transaction slips away or allow them to lay loose in your vehicle. Place them in a briefcase in an envelope until you get one and place them in the creditor's file in a locked cabinet. Keep records for a minimum of 10 years -- all receipts without exception. This is done in case a problem develops years down the road. Yes, you should have a creditor file for every creditor you do business with and start a new folder every January 1. Then box the prior year's items with your taxes in a locked room.

Do not carry such items as your birth certificate or social security cards with you every day unless necessary. Keep these items in a safe preferably, or at least a firebox. If you know someone is going to need a copy of such items as tax returns, or proof identity documents like your driver's license, etc. make the copies ahead of time. This will avoid the need for the firm's employee to leave the room with such information and be with such items outside of your sight. When you go to a restaurant be sure to note the name and appearance of employees who collect your credit card for payment and watch their actions while they have your card. If at all possible watch them until they return with the card. Ideally, you should be able to maintain sight of the employee 100% of the time from your table to the register. You will want to be observant but less than obvious in this endeavor. When a restaurant employee collects the card politely tell them to go to the register and straight back with no deviations of path. This avoids other patrons from seeing your account information and minimizes the possibility of thieves using a card imprint or palm scanner to collect the account holder's information. These tactics are common among well-organized criminals. Avoid leaving receipts on tables unattended. Be sure to hand them to restaurant employee so they are not left unattended.

When possible avoid giving information such as name, address, phone, etc., as many people will use things like raffles and similar events to gain basic information. Moreover, through public venues, public records and various sources they can gain other relevant and personal information about you. By minimizing who has the trivial information you avoid the ability for thieves to gain more specific information. Do not write checks out in front of others as this gives them the name of the bank, account and routing numbers of your institution and if they know you even remotely well they can gain other information needed. It is far more common that the victim knows the thieves. If you must buy something over the Internet, do not use Visa debit cards tied to your checking or savings account, use an actual credit card or even better use a prepaid disposable Visa or Master-card. You can get these at any number of retail stores, banks and similar locations. Only put a set amount on the card and change these often to avoid others from getting this information. This measure is taken so that if they do gain access to it, they will only get the very small balance left on the card as you only recharge the card when you are going to use it. These types of cards are great for an emergency as well as they are accepted anywhere that accepts credit cards and you can set the amount present on the card; but again, do not be excessive in the amount you put onto the card.

When a file has reached the 10-year mark and is ready to be destroyed use a shredder that cuts more than in strips but turns it into confetti. Then, fully-burn the confetti. This is critical, as once they have your name, address, date of birth and account number they can access everything else. Check each credit report at least annually. I personally recommend at least semi-annually. To avoid mailbox thieves I suggest you have your mail sent to a P.O Box rather than a physical address or office (boxes of this type with street addresses are available at places like the UPS store, Mailboxes, etc. and so on). Offices are actually worse than a residence as they commonly get a lot of traffic. I have found P.O. Boxes with street addresses are the best as only the one person with the code or key can retrieve the mail. There should be no more than two people with access and a single person is preferable. The fewer people with access the more secure you are.

I would also contact the Do Not Call registry for your state and the national Do Not Call registry. This will prevent scoundrels from marketing to you, as this is a common way for thieves to come off as legitimate to gather information on you. When you work with a business, avoid being put on marketing lists as these are often sold to others and the thieves sometimes are the purchasers of these lists. If you need the information have them send it by regular mail to your P.O. Box as noted above with a street address and give them limiting instructions as to what the information can be used for. Within this limiting instruction tell them they may not sell your information or provide it to any third party without your written consent. If this is violated they may be violating privacy, confidentiality laws and Hippa laws just to name a few examples depending on the type of vendor involved. These can be deemed federal crimes if they violate this directive. The only exception is most commonly those deemed to be required to be informed of such information in the providing of the service, but you will want to check this out before you hire such a firm for the service in question. By simply inquiring who will have access to such information.

Avoid leaving various statements or mail lying around out in the open as it lets thieves that you come in contact with know who you do business with and access to account information. If you use a computer for business and account tracking place a password and user ID system on the computer in order to use the computer. This may seem like overkill on a residence computer but I assure you it is not. I have even taken it a step further and purchased a VPN system for my computer. This enables the service to authenticate the site and verify not only its bona fides as legitimate, but test it to make sure it is secure and free from viruses, Trojans and similar spy-ware before actually connecting you to the site. These tools are the tools of the trade for thieves as these items allow the thieves to gain access to your computer, your past visiting locations and other vital information about you that may be on file with your Internet service provider. Electronic identity theft through the computer is becoming far more common than the traditional burglary due to the amount of anonymity it offers the thief.

Annually verify those that have information about you to be accurate and if access to such information is still warranted or should be terminated. I always urge people when selecting a vendor to determine the security systems and data storage systems protocols they have in place. If they have no electronic systems and they are solely a paper office these are by far the safest but rare in the age of computers. Along with this you will want to determine how they dispose of old data.

This chapter may come off as a sense of paranoia but it is not. Once you have been an identity theft victim these are the minimums. The key element of successful prevention is to not let others realize you are an identity theft victim, but simply implementing your prevention plan by keeping it low-key. One of the greatest elements in prevention is to not let others know you are watching. This allows thieves to feel comfortable and their actions to be clearly seen, which will in turn expose the scoundrels.

Chapter 11
The Do's, Don'ts & Hints

Up until this chapter I have told you my story and what to do and what not to do along the way. This chapter is designed to expound on these points and provide a more comprehensive list of do's and don'ts. Up until now I have only exposed those that I was faced with but there are many that will impact you that did not impact me. As I have stated throughout this book the process of identity recapture and the challenges you face will be specific and unique to you. We all have varying degrees of credit amounts, types, number of creditors and we all have various degrees of fraud perpetrated towards us as a result of the identity theft. Because of this, the things that are important to one identity theft victim will be completely different from that of another.

The purpose of this section is to try to give you some reference points to keep you on track within the recapture process and assist in preventing deviation from the plan or getting sidetracked from its effective implementation. The action plan outlined in the resource section is based within these guidelines to serve as a series of parameters to make sure you are not deviating from the action plan. However, the ultimate control is yours. The plan is simply that, a plan. If you choose to not follow it you are the only one who will pay the price. This plan is like so many others, it is simply best to follow it to the letter, as any attempt to deviate will only cause further delays and costs.

The Do's:

(1) File a formal objection with the bank regarding bank charges and fraudulent transactions.
(2) File a police report claiming identity theft.
(3) Secure a copy of your credit report from each of the credit reporting agencies individually.

(4) Decide if agency to be contacted regarding a creditor dispute is state or federal.

(5) You must dispute creditors in writing several times before enlisting regulator assistance; no exceptions.

(6) If they fail to comply with FCRA & Debt Collections Practices Acts (DCPA), force them to comply in writing in the timeline specified per the law (typically 30 days).

(7) Create an attorney list, by category (see hint list below for details before you start; you may have specific categories unique to your situation).

(8) Choose a legal service. This is not required but very helpful.

(9) Select and organize your letter templates in a simple format that can easily be altered for each creditor (see reference section).

(10) Do cite the laws. That is public information. Making your knowledge of their violation known is key to an effective letter.

(11) Do select the proper court to file a matter in. The proper court selection can be half the battle.

(12) Set up a separate account or fund for the legal challenges and only use these funds for identity theft related matters.

(13) Organize matters in order of priority (easy matters; district court and small claims; finally, civil and federal matters)

(14) Make final adjustments to priority order based on statutory clock.

(15) Determine those matters that are expected to need an attorney, then look at short list and determine attorney selection.

(16) Track progress by matter by plotting on a calendar by matter name.

(17) For those matters requiring an attorney, determine comp model and get agreement signed as you begin each matter, never after.

(18) Formulate an initial list of errors by creditor to dispute. Select one dispute reason per creditor for no more than five disputed creditors per bureau at a time.

(19) Make request for copy of credit report from the bureau, repeat process for each CRA as needed, also utilizing credit report updates received from bureaus following a dispute's completion (see resource section for contact and letter sample).

(20) Create system folders, and initial disputed creditor folders.

(21) Build credit when you do not need it so you have it when you do need it.

Good Foundation

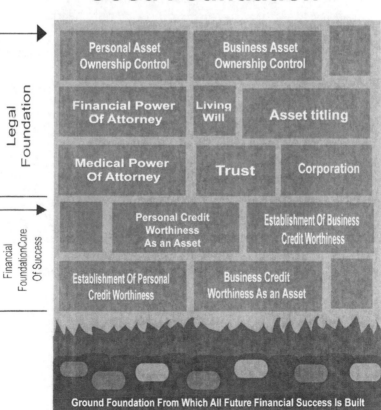

The Dont's:

(1) Be sure to make it a practice not to carry your social
     security card with you every day.

(2) Do not use a color copy, as this violates federal law,
     i.e., Patriot Act (black & white only).

(3) Refuse to pay anything resulting from fraud. Make no
     exceptions.

(4) Do not fill dispute letters with ambiguity or threats.
     This will not help the cause, and in fact will impede a
     dispute's request from being fulfilled.

(5) Do not hold yourself out as a legal professional.

(6) Do not work with an attorney without an agreement if
     you know they will represent you in court. This is OK,
     however, if the attorney is simply writing a letter for
     you but confirm the letter fee up front.

(7) Do not dispute more than five items per credit bureau
     at one time; no exceptions.

(8) Do not dispute the same creditor for the same reason
     two times in a row even if it's a valid claim.

(9) Do not wait to start this process, as delaying only
     wastes the statutory clock.

(10) Do not take government officials' word as the law of
     the land. If it's not in writing it's not binding.

(11) Do not deviate from the process of disputes or
     rebuilding, as it will only cause greater delay, greater
     damage and larger costs to get back on track.

(12) Do not file more than one dispute with the same credit
     bureau in the same 30-day period (30 days from their
     receipt of notice by certified mail).

Bad Foundation

The Hints:

Never throw anything away for a minimum of at least ten years. If it's a report such as a police report, or directly related to identity theft then retain it forever, no exceptions.

Be persistent but polite, as when you attempt to get a police report many times your request will be denied.

Make sure they do not simply realign the account and reissue a new debit card and pin. Rather, insist that they issue a fully new account, debit card and pin assigned to a new account number and that the old information is not realigned under the new account but that the old account is marked closed, zero balance per consumer request.

Make certain to get the police report number, officer's card and date when report will be available, so that a copy can be retrieved. Once available, procure a copy of the report and make several copies of it. Organization right from the start is key to long-term success in recapturing your identity.

So that you do not need to carry your social security card and other items with you regularly while fighting your identity theft, place a copy of your driver's license and social security card on a single sheet of paper. Make copies, as every time you make a formal request this will need to be attached. If you have an updated address on the back be sure to make the copy noted above and then recopy it with the backside also included on the single page and use this as the master copy.

Regardless of what the institution says they do not care about you no matter how long you have done business with them. I will cover this in greater detail later on. The bank's sole purpose is to minimize potential liability for the events at all costs.

Determine if it is a state or federal matter specifically before contacting agency.

Be sure to do a series of disputes and inquire yourself before enlisting assistance, as they are not your personal staff but are to be used when you cannot get an agency to do their job.

Manage the closing of accounts and account types (when, how and how often). Excessive account closings will cause your score to drop dramatically if done over a short period of time or if the number of accounts in credit types is insufficient in number (ideally, three revolving accounts and 4 installment loans open at all times).

Per the FCRA & Debt Collections Practices Acts there are specific requirements and timelines. If they fail to comply with these the items in question must be removed without exception. In general terms 30 days from receipt of your request with limited exceptions.

Whether or not you use a legal service or have a firm on retainer you need to create a list of attorneys that handle the following areas of law. This is only a basic list and you may find that you need a couple of additional categories specific to your situation.

- FCRA Attorney
- Contract law & collections attorney
- Civil action attorney

Legal services are fine but be sure you know the contract inside and out and also be sure to use one that offers an unlimited number of matters; otherwise you are wasting your money.

Only use proven letters, as ambiguity is your enemy in a dispute letter.

When responding to a motion or other requests do so in writing by certified mail or process-server only.

Be sure to track everything by calendar so nothing is overlooked, as every detail matters.

The details, time lines, and response format are the keys to success in the recapture process.

Be sure to provide proof of identity with all submissions or they will be stalled or ignored altogether. Only answer relevant questions asked but respond to all requests regardless.

Manage your credit profile in terms the types of creditors shown, number of creditors shown, age of accounts shown, etc. Having the right mix will allow you to maximize your score. There are firms that can aid you with this (Google "search credit optimization" or visit www.planningwithmerit.com's membership area for possible resources).

Chapter 12
NOW WHAT?

O nce you have been a victim of identity theft and you have completed the removal of the false information, the common question then becomes: now what? The answer is simply you must rebuild your credit. An effective and strong credit score is composed of a mix of creditor types ranging from revolving accounts, installment loans, mortgages and numerous others. Additionally, within these general categories are sub categories such as department store revolving accounts, traditional credit card revolving accounts, secured revolving accounts, car loans, signature loans... the list is rather long and varying by person, region of the country and related variables.

HOW TO REBUILD CREDIT AFTER IDENTITY THEFT

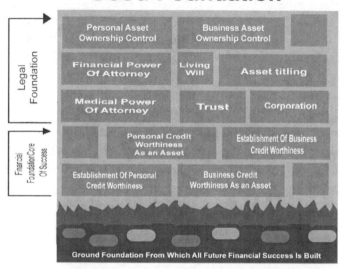

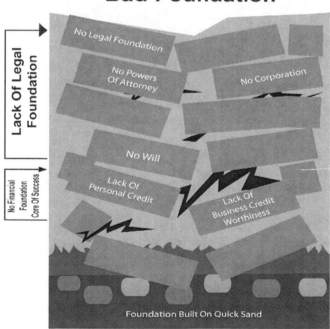

Having said this the question becomes where do I start to rebuild my credit? The general answer is different for each person. However, I will now outline what needs to be accomplished in general terms. Based on the items that are positively reporting on your various reports, you will then need to decide which items you need to focus on first. One of the determining factors is which positive accounts are reporting on each respective bureau by type of credit and how much longer they will continue to report. Creditors that are paid in full will continue to report on your credit report for up to a maximum of seven years following the date of being paid in full. If you have an open account with a balance that is in good standing, the seven-year clock on this account has not started yet. This will begin once paid in full and/or closed.

Equally as important as the types of the accounts are the age of the account, the remaining balance on the account, the original amount of credit given and many other variables. However, rather than getting into the minutia of trying to outline these points my objective here is to give the reader a general understanding of what they are looking for and what impact this general model will have on your credit score. Never apply for more than two credit applications of any kind in any 30-day period if at all possible, though there will be times it will not be able to be helped. If considering credit find out what bureau the creditor uses and get the report yourself and then meet with the prospective lender to see the likelihood of approval before actually applying. This will minimize unneeded inquires on your report and reduce your score reductions for unapproved application inquires. In an optimal situation you first want to make sure that what is reporting on each credit bureau is reporting correctly. Secondly, if you have positive creditors that are reporting to some credit bureaus but not on all, use the sample letter in the resource section to request that this information be reported to the other credit bureaus. Occasionally, there may be a nominal fee for this but it is well worth the cost. I have personally found that I have not been charged any fees for these reporting requests. However, some people are. In most cases this is determined by the creditor, not the credit bureaus themselves. Essentially, the firm you are asking to report is passing the cost to do so onto you. This may seem unfair in some respects and you would be right but being charged is a rare occurrence unless the creditor to be reported is a real bottom feeder. I will get into creditor analysis a bit later in this chapter.

Once the existing positive accounts have been reported to those credit reporting agencies that the creditor agrees to report to (optimally this would be all but this will not always be possible) as a matter of company practice or per your written request, they have complied with the law. I say the only requirement is for a creditor to report to a credit bureau but the creditors are not in fact required to report to all credit bureaus. Moreover, in some instances they are not required to report to any credit reporting agency of any kind and is deemed at the creditor's discretion to report. Next you will want to make sure that all of your personal information is correct. This includes but is not limited to the spelling of name, name variations, current address, past address, current phone number, date of birth, employer and various components of these entries (you only want one version of your name, address, phone and other similar information to appear; no exceptions). The devil is in the details. You see, if you have duplicate listings of items, invalid items, false dates, etc. this can do two things. It can affect your score but more importantly it can impact your ability to get credit in the future. When you apply for credit many times the firm that is looking to extend you credit will verify what you listed on the application with that which is shown in the report. Things like wrong to and from dates with employers, incorrect employers, false address information, typos and similar entries can cause the creditor to not extend credit as they may feel you are lying to them or intentionally committing fraud yourself. It is critical to remember as I have stated previously, once you have been a victim of ID theft you will have to continue to prove you are legitimate. The easiest way to do that is to make sure that duplications, errors in spellings, dates and similar items are not present and these are some of the easiest credit score points to regain. In this regard also be prepared for the false information to reappear from time to time as it is given by the creditors that you have or have not done business with in the past or are doing business with currently. They may have the error in their system so expect to have to address some items more than once. I recommend that you make the correction requests of this nature at the credit source so you can then go to the source and have it corrected fully. Many times this will solve the problem fully and only a few will need to be addressed multiple times. Amongst the most common ones that typically reappear are things like improper addresses, past addresses, typo errors, aliases, etc. that you do not use (only use a single variation for all data elements for all credit applications past or present, no exceptions). Duplicates of these items must be eliminated. Even the slightest errors such as using the word APT, unit, etc. when not in the official address must be eliminated.

The goal is to have a trade line appear that is active and at least 24 months long in duration or longer, but 70% of installment account points are achieved at 24 months. If it is a revolving account you always want to maintain an open account perpetually with a small balance (optimally 7% at time of bureau reporting each month). Paying the bill off in full every month, while a good financial decision, hurts your credit score, so be prudent in this regard. The flip side of that is you do not want to have the account maxed out either (ideally use as you wish throughout month but no more than 7% is best on the date the account reports to the bureaus each month). The goal is to never have the balance present on the account exceed more than 30-40% of the total line available. Thirty-nine percent is the absolute max. A reduction in score will occur though it's typically nominal. However, if unavoidable in the short-term, plan to rectify this matter as soon as possible. And if you go above this utilization rate your score will be hurt in terms of points available for the trade line account in question. This will also severely hurt the trade line category portfolio (i.e., revolving, installment and so on) for any amounts in excess of the 39% both in terms of score and acquiring credit. Your goal is to have 2-3, no more than 4 revolving accounts of different types. Meaning perhaps a credit union Visa or Master-card (national credit unions preferably), and a traditional credit card such as a Visa or Master-card (national, regional or community bank issued). You can have more but be careful. Once you get above four revolving accounts your score is impacted negatively (avoid retail department store credit cards and gas cards as these are deemed finance cards and only receive a fraction of the available points for these card types). If you decide to close an account do not close too many at the same time as this will hurt your score as well. Close an account if not being used but do not close multiple accounts at the same time as it will reduce the average age of your accounts for the account category (i.e., revolving, installment, etc.) and damage your overall credit score severely. If a preferable credit card type as noted above, use it and keep a small balance on it and make the minimum payment and repeat as needed a couple times a year. For more detailed information in this regard (see www.planningwithmerit.com's membership area for possible resources).

Installment loans
The next type of credit is installment loans. The long-term goal is to have at least four installment loans open and reporting at all times. Even if paid off, former installment loans add depth to the report and value. This is generally pretty easy to maintain though it may be difficult immediately following the identity theft. Having a car loan, a mortgage and a couple of smaller installment loans, in most cases can be accomplished. Especially if an asset is involved making it a secured loan like a car loan or house loan secured by the asset. If you do not have an asset like this you can create one a couple of different ways. Take some cash and put it into a CD or a savings account and then use the asset to secure the loan. Yes, you are using your own money to secure an installment loan and paying money to a firm to do it. However, what they are giving you is a secured credit loan and establishing a credit relationship to build on. This same idea can be used to secure a credit card if you have difficulties. Again take cash or an asset like a CD and pledge it to secure a credit card. You will want to maintain a balance

on it so it reports in a way to affect your score positively but maintain the 7-10% or less as a rule. If you do not like making payments but need an installment loan another way to do this is to borrow funds, secured or unsecured, in a balloon loan. Borrow $1,000 and put it in your savings account. When the balloon payments come do which is usually in intervals of 90 days, 6 months, or 12 months you will pay back the loan and the interest due. You then repeat the process. The goal is to each time increase the amount. The only other way is to buy an asset like a car and pay really high interest and then 12 or 24 months later refinance the car for better terms once you have completed the various options noted above in regards to various credit types. You can easily have your credit score back to excellent status in 12 to 24 months if you have a little funds to establish secured accounts. Or perhaps you have a lender you have an established relationship with which will work with you to incrementally do loans with you to allow them to report. Credit unions are commonly known for this if you have an established history, but do not count on this. Having said this make sure to spread your business around a little with different firms, but giving a slightly larger portion of business to a firm that is willing to work with you is certainly a good idea.

CREDIT REPORTING AGENCIES & FORMULAS
The FICO (Fair Isaac Corporation) company's scoring models are used in the U.S., Canada, Mexico, the United Kingdom, Ireland, Poland, Sweden, Turkey, Bahrain, Saudi Arabia, South Africa, Russia, Singapore, Republic of Korea, Thailand, Taiwan, Brazil, Peru, and Panama. Each of these countries have enacted laws in regards to identity theft, credit scoring and credit reporting agencies. However, some have stronger laws than others. While this is the case, the general structure has been consistent for the most part in terms of the formula that was originally created. Be sure, however, to recognize that in many countries this was modified to fit the products and services available within it and related political structures. The United States is one of the largest but also has some of the most comprehensive laws and scoring systems. This is primarily due to the fact that the United States has the largest range of

products available to consumers in terms of types of credit. To
aid in the general understanding of all this, we will focus on
the United States model for our conversation. The U.S. model
is structured as follows:

    35%   Payment History –

    30%   Credit Utilization –

    15%   Length of Credit History –

    10%   Types of Credit Used (installment, revolving,
                 consumer finance, mortgage) –

    10%   Recent search for credit and/or amount of
                 credit obtained recently –

———————————

    100%

ATTEMPTS TO KEEP THE SCORING MODEL IN A STATE OF FLUX

While this is the game plan also realize that the credit
reporting agencies are trying as of the writing of this book to
increase the credit score range and some have already gotten
this approved and it simply has not gone into effect yet. What
this essentially means is if you have a 720 credit score today
and the new guideline formulas are inserted your core may
be reduced to 620 due to no fault of yours. This is another
example of the dirty tactics the credit bureaus are playing to
create more client lists of people with lower scores so that they
can sell to creditors looking to offer credit to the safer credit
risks but want to justify charging you a higher rate. You would
say this is morally wrong and you would be right. To promote
this new corrupt initiative the credit bureaus are trying to
roll out to the creditors a new scoring system, which most are
calling it advantage scoring. The scoring readjusts the weight

given to various things from credit type and outstanding balances to the weight given to a 30-day late reporting even if the late was more than 24 months in the past. This alters the period in which prior inquiries are counted and countless other similar items. The goal is to keep your score down to keep their profits up. This is one of the leading reasons I wrote this book: my experience following my identity theft in this regard in terms of intentional score manipulation towards me based on the product being acquired through credit. This can be a car or some other specific credit type through a changing of the weight given to such loan types from the standard model.

The current FICO score is between 300 and 850, exhibiting a skewed interpretation with 60% of scores nearly right between 650 and 799. According to FICO the median score is 723. Once the new adjustments are implemented this will pull this average down to a 620 median score or lower. This is accomplished by adding numerous enhancements to the scoring system. These include but are not limited to raising the top number from the current 850 to 950. This results in everyone's score being reduced. Adding enhancements to the calculation for the presence of the sub-prime mortgage market, this adjustment penalizes those that pay on time by reducing the score due to those partaking in the sub-prime mortgage market. In the last couple years the firms have incrementally begun to unveil their goal of redefining the model. This redefining, once accepted as commonplace will be altered regularly to fit the changing economic times. This is exactly what the scoring method was originally designed to prevent. It was designed to evaluate an individual's credit worthiness based on past activity without being impacted by others. The credit reporting agencies in short are attempting to implement social policy as relates to credit availability. Several states have tried to take this approach and have received notable pressure to not proceed while others were successful. Among these is the implementation on a state by state basis of credit scores to determine the cost of such items as auto insurance and utility costs. The outcome is varied from region to region and from product topic to product topic. Because of this fact it is critical that one stays aware of the changes and the status of one's credit report. The unveiling of the advantage scoring will enable lenders to filter things as they see fit and in some instances legally discriminate. However, certain items have been forbidden from being used in the formula calculation. These include but are not limited to such items as such as race, religion, national origin, sex, and marital status. Another requirement is that if a person is denied for credit they must be notified in writing as to why. To make this uniform the credit reporting agencies have developed a series of codes for these decisions. This forces the reporting agency to use a predetermined set of criteria in the denial process. The thought here by legislators was that this would enable the borrower to fix the problem and then reapply. A series of laws have been enacted to ensure that the availability of credit is made fairly. These laws include the following, and this is only a partial list and is only a sampling of those at the federal level as there are a huge number on an individual state basis as well. However, given that our conversation is meant as an overview I have focused on the applicable federal laws, but I do encourage you to look at those relating to your specific state.

- Fair Credit Reporting Act (FCRA)

- Debt Collection Practices Act (DCPA)

- Equal Credit Opportunity Act (ECOA)

- Interstate commerce laws

-Confidentiality & privacy laws

- Civil Rights laws

- Billing Act

It is critical that you understand that each credit reporting agency has placed its own minor adjustments to the model to come up with its score for you. You have multiple scores as an individual. These include but are not limited to Experian, Equifax, Transunion and numerous others.

In recent years there were firms that would aid you to temporarily raise your score by adding trade lines to your report that portrayed favorable ratios of balance to line availability to raise your score. But you did not actually have access to the actual line of credit in most cases. In an effort to prevent manipulations of these types, enhancements began to be added in 2008 as a counter-measure in this regard. Again, this is an example of the credit reporting agencies taking away the consumer's ability to manipulate the score. However, they then subsequently enabled the people using the score, the lenders, to do just that. This is a double standard that must be understood as the credit game is ever changing and only those on top of their game have the best scores. Scores can impact the job you receive, the credit you receive, and even the rates you pay for auto insurance. I urge all to have a basic understanding as noted above of the scoring system and then simply keep abreast of changes that may impact you as they come into play.

The short to do list:

- Maintain your personal information accurately.
- Maintain 4 installment loans comprised of 1 mortgage, 1 vehicle loan and two other installment loans.
- Maintain 3 quality revolving accounts maintain 7-10% balance. The older the account the better.
- Manage the number of inquiries on each bureau to under 3 on an annual basis optimally.

For a specific action plan enlist an optimization specialist, through Google search or through www.planningwithmerit. com's membership section (the shortcut for those who want to hire credit optimization and related services).

Critical Budgeting Basics

To prevent one from repeating the process and breaking the cycle that the creditors want to keep you in I have included this general outline to aid you in formulating your finances. For every dollar you bring in via income the government takes ranging from 15% to 50%(taxes) depending on your income level once you factor in state, local and federal income taxes paid. This allows you to arrive at your net income, the amount you receive in your check each week. These tax deductions are after you have contributed to paying for health insurance, retirement accounts and, as applicable, payroll taxes.

When you apply for a loan in most cases, though, they will use your gross income before taxes and insurance is deducted. This often causes people to spend more money than they can actually afford in regards to debt payments. To prevent this I would outline the following game plan and this will work for any person regardless of income level; the numbers will simply be different. The goal is to make sure that your monthly debt obligations never exceed 30-38% of your gross income, and optimally total debt service payments should not exceed roughly 19% in a perfect world. Essentially, if you make $40,000 per year then you should spend no more than $12,000 annually or $1,000 per month in debt payments (optimally $633.33 in monthly payments). These debt payments include such items as cars, credit cards, mortgages, etc. The leading problem with this is most people do not know how to get on such a plan so I will outline this below in simplistic terms to aid you.

Take your gross income before taxes, then subtract the cost of health insurance, and a minimum of 20% for a retirement plan or until maxed out, whichever occurs first. Second, try to manage your deductions and exemptions so that you get very little tax refunds back and do not have to pay in, essentially a zero sum game in terms of taxes owed or over-paid, though a small refund is better than paying in. In the beginning this will be tough to get used to as it will reduce your monthly check. However, you have to learn to pay yourself first and putting a minimum of 20% in retirement is a must if you want to retire and this also reduces your taxes (what you invest in will be covered in a later book in the series). The retirement element needs to be implemented from the beginning to take advantage of time long term. This should only be delayed if debt service is above 39% of your income annually.

This will then give you a new net income and yes in the beginning it will be less than you are used to but understand that this is temporary, as you will see. Now we return to the subject of debt. You need a dependable car, a place to live, etc. but these debt payments should not exceed 30% in an optimal situation and no more than 39% in a less favorable position. If you are above this 39% figure you are living beyond your means, and you must cut expenses. While most banks like less debt some will let you run this up to as high as 50% but this should be avoided as their goal is to keep you in debt as you are the bank's income source. If the debt service is under 19% then you are on track currently, the lower the better but never 0%. This is the simplest plan to follow but it simply takes making a decision.

The remaining 60-70% of your net income is to be used as you wish after you have done the following things. You need to contribute monthly to a savings account or money market account until you have saved an amount equal to 12 months of net income and preferably 12 months of gross income instead. This will take time so do not be discouraged. This can only be done though if your debt is not above the 39% max. If your debt is above this level reduce debt first. To reduce debt, sell the toys with payments and sell toys that are paid for that cost to operate if you have more than one. With he money you save monthly from these sales then take 50% of savings and apply to remaining debt and take the remaining 50% and break into two 25% funds. The first is to begin the savings plan noted above and the second 25% fund is for future purchases. The future purchases fund is to be used when it comes time to buy a new car, fix a furnace, etc. You want to always continue to fund this even when you think you do not need to, as this will enable you to pay cash for the next car, which I do not recommend (rather, use these funds to establish your desired car payment within 19% debt or less overall). However, you should pay cash for the next furnace (it is recommended to pay cash for these types of items) and not require such purchases to be put on credit. This is a fund that you will always fund and eventually will be used to buy future toys with cash, and operating funds for toys and vacation funds. The goal is to eliminate debt beyond optimal levels (19-30%) and live on what you make, and use the excess to put away for future purchases.

The purpose is so you can earn interest on your money and put your money to work for you rather than working to pay for the use of someone else's money. This may mean cutting back on your lifestyle temporarily so be prepared. Items that are to also come out of the 70% are non-debt related required items. These include such things as food, utilities, gas for the car, vacation fund, entertainment fund, etc. Items purchased or to be purchased in 12 months or less come out of the 70% and future purchases come out of the fund noted above. This may sound tough and in the beginning it will be to teach you to live within your means. I have provided a budget worksheet for you to create your current existing budget. This will help you determine where cuts can be made. You can then use a new budget sheet as you eliminate debt. Let's say you sell a toy and eliminate a $200 monthly bill. You then take the $200 monthly saving and allocate it into the 50%, 25%, 25% format noted above until you pay off the next creditor, and then repeat. You will find out that whatever terms your creditor debt was on, you will cut it by 40-50% in terms of length. What this means is look at the number of payments you will not have to make and multiply it by the monthly payment and this will tell you how much interest you saved. The interest savings will go to pay-off the next creditor.

The largest creditor is generally one's mortgage but in this item's regard you can typically take a 30-year mortgage down to roughly 27.5 years or so. If you apply other techniques such as taking the monthly payment and dividing it into two payments, the first half two weeks before its due and the second half on the actual due date, you end up saving interest. This is because not only the second two weeks payments was applied to a lower balance (meaning more on the loan's principal balance). This works the same way as the credit cards but because most mortgages are simple interest (meaning each payment is comprised of principal and interest, with more of the earlier payments going to pay interest first) in nature you end up dramatically reducing the term. If you were to simply double your payments through credit bills being eliminated and applied this to your mortgage without the shortcut noted above you can take a 30-year mortgage and pay it off in five years. If you apply the bi-weekly system noted above as well it can be even shorter. The key is discipline.

To keep your credit in good standing you want to have balances on credit but simply consistently low balances. As I stated before do not pay them off 100%, always keep a small balance. Charge something such as gas for the month and pay off the lion's share but not all and then repeat (again optimally 7-10% at time of monthly reporting to respective credit bureaus).

BUSINESS OWNERS & CREDIT
If you are a business owner listen up and listen good. You do not want to use your personal credit lines to build your business. You want to set up an entity and then establish credit under the entity by itself without personal guarantees. This is commonly referred to as non-recourse debt. Even if the credit in the company name is secured by an asset it is only non-recourse if you as the business owner do not have to guarantee it. If you set up a profile properly this can take place pretty easily. There are firms to establish this for you for a fee. The cost for this type of a reputable service is about $1,600 on average to as little as $400 for do it yourself programs; depending on the client's involvement level this can be more or less. Do not simply use the business credit bureaus' systems to do this, as they are not bound by many laws of the FCRA, which are on the personal credit side. When you establish business credit initially, you will start with items commonly

called "trade credit," allowing you to buy from a certain vendor or stores. Once you establish these for 3-4 months you will move on to items like gas cards and repeat the process, in addition to continued use of the trade credit. Then you will secure your first business Visa and finally you will move into installment loans. Again in each instance securing an account, using it, paying it off, letting the payment report and repeating the process in simple terms (see www.planningwithmerit.com on book relating to business credit).

The process to build business credit can take 6-12 months. The amount you receive will depend on the particulars of the company's profile and the age of the business. I bring this up because if you are business owner like I was and endure identity theft it can impact things much harder and much harsher if you do not have a separate business credit profile. If tied to your personal credit it can not only destroy your livelihood, you can be forced to liquidate at huge discounts and be held responsible for any balance remaining in the end. This will destroy your family's future. I learned this the hard way and had to liquidate several partnerships; this can occur perhaps when it is not the best time to sell specified assets. Forced sales are sold at huge discounts that means lost money for you even if it covers the debt owed. Financial leverage of assets is powerful but it is a double-edged sword so manage it closely. The key way to do this is to make sure business entities assets and liabilities are separate from your personal assets and liabilities. No exceptions.

Also, if you are guarantor or are using recourse debt for your business this will reduce how much credit you can get for personal credit purposes like buying a home, car, etc. Separating these two is the key and then you can simply use your high personal credit score to get better terms in regards to your business lines when you get to the cash lines of credit stage that are over one million. You will need to manage the business credit reports even closer than the personal credit bureaus as they are not bound by many of the same restrictions and blemish can destroy the business credit profile with that bureau forever so do it right and build it over time. However, some of the same principles apply, so maintain a balance but not a huge one and pay it down but not off (unless required per creditor agreement to do so) each month. You should also have funds that if you wanted to you could put in a money market or savings account. The business budget should follow the same formulas in your business budgeting as noted in your personal budget, but rather than retirement it is reinvestment and you can use the same budget sheet to manage the balances. The key difference with the business budget is that instead of retirement its reinvestment or cash reserves for your business. The money you pay yourself is an expense for the business. However, unlike the personal budget you pay the bills first and then pay yourself. The easiest way to deal with this ebb and flow is to put yourself on a weekly check and then if money is available at year-end or at a specified time pay a bonus to yourself. The salary figure is what you use as your figures for your personal income budget.

If you are a business owner you have two budgets, one for the business and the one for you personally. Never blend the two. If the company needs a loan treat it like one to the company, as a capital investment and write the company a check and agreement. The better option is to use other people's money as once you have a credit profile the terms will be more favorable to take this approach of business capital needs. You can also use a company asset as collateral to secure a loan. If you use other people's money (OPM) this can then report on the business' credit reports. This builds a track record. The longer and better the track record the better the size, interest rate charged and other terms of credit available. Once this business credit becomes extremely strong and large lines of credit are available you can if you so choose lend the money for even greater profits. It is very common for a business owner to come into an opportunity for a short-term investment that they know is a good deal if they only had the money to act on it. This business credit gives you that ability. This is the business putting its money and borrowing power to work for profit. This is allowing your money to work for you instead of you working for your money (you become the bank). A warning though, always maintain the ratios noted above, no exception regardless of the opportunity. Remember you have cash reserves for a reason, if it's not enough available on lines. However, only do this once you have the 12 months safety net in place.

Creditor Analysis
Creditors can be analyzed in many ways. The purpose here is not to get into the analysis process but more importantly how to avoid the bottom feeders. The creditor's minimum and maximum credit score tolerance, if known, are a key indicator. If this information is not known as is the case for most clients you want to look at the interest rates being charged. What to compare this to is the prime rate, which you can get from any financial publication source for your region. Typically A paper vendors will charge 1-3% above prime depending on the type of account being sought...revolving, installment, etc. If an asset secures the loan, this will be only slightly above prime. If your credit is deemed B grade credit then you can expect the rates to start at the high-end of the aforementioned range and group another 1% or so. If your credit is deemed C grade then you can expect the rate to be double-digit for certain and this will vary greatly by the credit type and other related terms. The lender may have a higher interest rate but better payment options, balance transfer options and other variables of this type. If you are in D grade credit this is when you will for certain be using guaranteed loans and lower amounts of credit initially but will grow over time. If you are forced to start in the D grade plan, switch vendors at the 24-month mark at the latest as credit improves.

Another point to consider is the reputation of the firm involved. While each creditor type has its place in the marketplace do not allow another person to set your credit grade permanently as they will always pick a grade lower than you actually deserve to protect their profit margin. While the purpose of this book is not to promote any one vendor, I will try to outline some current examples of creditors that have programs in each of the four credit grades noted above.

Examples of A grade :
will be your local regional bank or national bank branch in the area.

Examples of B grade:
are going to be slightly larger regional banks in the area and surrounding states only, or banks that have a strong branch presence in your region. This is where most national banks try to market themselves, even those that do not have a large brick and mortar presence.

Examples of C grade:
are going to be the bottom feeders that have huge marketing budgets and offer the off the wall programs in TV commercials and similar venues by mail.

Examples of D grade:
are the national banks and finance companies that have a reputation for being scoundrels. I could name countless examples of these. They tend to be finance companies that have a national presence or national banks that lend based on extremely low credit scores and charge extremely high interest and fee structures.

These are the lenders that market to the lowest common denominators when relating to credit. I urge you to do a creditor search online based on the credit type you are looking for whether it is revolving or installment and see what lenders appear for your area. Then refine the search in such a way as to make it more general and the larger names will appear. These large names will most commonly be your C & D vendors unless it is a vendor that only services you specific area. You then can check to see their niche client types and determine where they fall in the scoring spectrum. You then place yourself score wise on the spectrum and you will have a short list of vendors that you can use at that point in time. The list of vendors and your score will change, and as the score improves so will the vendors. The purpose of this section is simply to give you the basics in evaluation. You want to look into detail about a potential vendor's background or determine if they are a firm in the group you have to choose from that you want to do business with. The purpose of the above analysis is to provide you with ways to give you the short list to evaluate your current needs for a loan type at the time.

The personal consulting team

You have two consulting teams. You have your personal team and the team for your business. The personal team is comprised of numerous people and they may change from time to time as your situation changes. The team is typically composed of your legal team as noted in this book relating to your identity theft matters and the attorney you use for general matters, estate planning and other similar legal matters. This includes the property and casualty agent, the financial planner for estate planning and other insurance needs and your investment advisor. The estate planner and the investment advisor may be the same firm but may or may not be the same person. Additionally, you will want to have an accountant, preferably a CPA (Certified Public Accountant). You may have other team members depending on your personal situation. These could include and are not limited to a house management team for things like lawn care service, housekeeper, possibly a bookkeeper, etc. All of these have to be included if applicable in the budget.

The business consulting team

The business management team is most commonly set up like a board of directors and functions the same way as the above group but may be contracted team members instead of employees. Some team members are not commonly on the personal team but can be team members like bookkeeper, accounts payable person, accounts receivable person, etc. These team members are in addition to those in categories as outlined in the personal group. One might ask why am I bringing this up in an identity theft book. The answer is simple: identity theft begins, ends and is recovered from through the use of these team members and budgets. If you try to run the course without a budget plan it is only a matter of time before you are back trying to start again. The budget and the use of experts in the various areas at varying levels of support based on your situation are the key to your long-term success. Building your business financial house and your personal financial house all begin with a foundation and credit is the brick of that foundation. Those that have experienced identity theft have a crack in the foundation but it can be repaired through the identity theft recapture system and proper use of budgets. If ignored eventually the house will fall; it is simply a matter of time. This book is the first step in repairing that crack, through recovering from identity theft and establishing strong personal and business credit if applicable. Once the recapture is complete then comes the rebuilding and maintaining stage. This is a stage once reached that must be managed and maintained (failing to maintain your financial house chips at its financial foundation's strength) on an ongoing basis forever.

MERRITT & ASSOCIATES INC." Planning with Merit"

Name_____

Six Month Cash Flow Summary   Date_____

Please go back six months in your checkbook or receipts and fill in
the exact amounts.

	Month 1	Month 2	Month 3	Month 4	Month 5	Month 6	Once a year
Expenses							
House/Rent							
Electricity							
Natural Gas/Propane							
Telephone							
Water/Sewer/Trash							
Taxes							
Car Payments							
Gas							
Car Insurance							
Car Maintenance							
Food							
Clothing							
Medical/Dental							
Drugs/Medicine							
Laundry/Cleaning							
Gifts							
Contributions							
Haircuts							
House Maintenance							
Medical Insurance							
Disability Insurance							
Life Insurance							
Savings							
Vacation Savings							

	Month 1	Month 2	Month 3	Month 4	Month 5	Month 6	Once a year
Investment Savings							
Credit Card-Total Owed							
1. $							
2. $							
3. $							
4. $							
5 $							
6. $							
7. $							
Adult Continuing Ed.							
Primary Ed.							
Secondary Ed.							
College Ed.							
Newspaper/Periodicals							
Entertainment							
Babysitting							
Cash							
TOTAL OUTLAY							
Net Paycheck							
Net Paycheck							
Net Investment Income							
TOTAL NET INCOME							
BALANCE + or -							

Chapter 13 RESOURCE DIRECTORY

FOR ADDITIONAL VENDOR SERVICES (SEE):

www.planningwithmerit.com

MEMBERS ONLY AREA:

- Creditor dispute services
- Inquiry dispute services
- Credit optimization services

(Numerous other effective services on an as needed basis):

(prescreened to save time and money) GO TO:

www.planningwithmerit.com (member's only section)

(for those who choose to not do it their self)

I. Credit reporting agency contact information (cra):

PRIMARY TRADITIONAL CREDIT BUREAUS:

Experian: 1-888-397-3742 (Automated request line, request report by phone)

Mailing address: **Experian**
                        P.O Box 9701
                        Allen, TX 75013

Trans Union: 1-866-887-2673 (Automated request line, request report by phone)

Mailing address: **Trans Union Consumer Relations**
                        P.O Box 200
                        Chester, PA 19022

Equifax: 1-800-685-1111 (Automated request line, request report by phone)

Mailing address::   **Equifax Information Services LLC.**
                        P.O Box 105314
                        Atlanta, GA 30348

You may also call 1-877-322-8228 to acquire all THREE with a single call (Central Distribution Number)

For those who wish to perform the acquisition of the reports online they may do so by also going to
www.annualcreditreport.com

ALL OF THE ABOVE ITEMS ARE FREE OF CHARGE ONCE PER YEAR FROM EACH SOURCE

www.myfico.com   (costs but typically should be reviewed at least once per year)

IF YOU WANT YOUR CREDIT SCORES MAY BE ACQUIRED FOR A FEE AT 1-877-726-7311

Note: only scores acquired from MyFico.com are true credit scores, all others have been filtered in some way as noted earlier.

ALTERNATE CREDIT REPORTING AGENCIES & INDUSTRY REPORTING AGENCIES:

Chex Systems: 1-800-513-7125
(Automated request line, request report by phone)

Mailing address: **Chex Systems, Inc.**
                        7805 Hudson road, Suite 100
                        Woodbury, MN 55125

You may also call customer service at 1-800-513-7125 Choose option 1 for English, then option 5 for customer service assistance

OR

You may also call and hear instructions at: 1-800-428-9623

www.consumerdebit.com (this site has a great deal of information on this CRA)

TO LOCATE A NON CHEX SYSTEMS AFFILIATED BANK:

Go to www.chexsystemsvictims.com/about my list

You will want to check with the banks to confirm their status has not changed but these are firms not affiliated with Chex Systems, Inc, reporting and are the preferred choice due to this fact.

ALTERNATE CREDIT REPORTING AGENCIES & INDUSTRY REPORTING AGENCIES CONTINUED:

• **SCAN** (Shared Check Authorization Network):
       You may also call SCAN at: 1-800-262-7771
       (Follow automated prompts that apply)

• **Telecheck:**
   Mailing address: Telecheck:
                             5550-A Peachtree Parkway, Suite 600
                             Norcross, GA 30092

You may also call Telecheck at: 1-800-209-8186

OR

Go to: www.telecheck.com
click on appropriate green box along right hand side near the top

• **Certegy/Equifax:**
   Mailing address: Certegy Check Services, Inc.
                             11601 Roosevelt Boulevard
                             Saint Petersburg, FL 33716

You may also call Certegy at: 1- 800-437-5120
You may call Certegy customer care at: 1-800-352-5970

OR

www.certegy.com

• **CLUE, INC.**: 1-866-312-8076
  (Automated request line, request report by phone)
  Mailing address::   Clue, Inc.
                         Consumer Disclosure Center
                         P.O Box 105295
                         Atlanta, GA 30348

You may also call Auto & Home Owners at: 1-866-312-8076
(Note same as Auto & home owners below simply another
branding name)

• **MIB** (Medical Information Bureau):
  Mailing address: MIB, Inc.
                        50 Braintree Hill Park, Suite 400
                        Braintree, MA 02184-8734
                        You may also call MIB at:
                        1- 866-692-6901

THOSE CREDIT REPORTING AGENCIES LISTED
BELOW CAN BE REACHED BY PHONE AND FOLLOW
TIIE PROMPTS:

• **International Check Service**: You may also call International
  Check Service at: 1-800-526-5380

• **Auto & Home Owners**: You may also call Auto & Home
  Owners at: 1-866-312-8076

• **Work Place Solutions**: You may also call Work Place Solutions
  at: 866-312-8075

• **CHECK CENTER/CROSS CHECK**: You may also call
  cross check at: 1-800-843-0760

• **LEXIS/NEXUS**: You may also call Lexis/Nexus at: 1-877-
  448-5732

(Request address for your geographic region if you need to
make a request or dispute by mail)

II. Credit reporting agencies that can help you with the fight against non reporting items:

• **PRBC**: For assistance you may use online form or call:
  1-800-884-4397

OR

You may Contact & Enroll in **PRBC** at www.prbc.com
(Note you will need a vendor's assistance as of recent but no cost to either you or the vendor)

III. Possible credit monitoring services

• **Credit Check Total**:
  www.creditchecktotal.com
  Phone: 1-866-506-7894

• **Privacy Guard**:
  www.privacyguard.com
  Phone: 1-800-374-8273

These are just to name few. Be sure to check as these organizations run specials and discounted prices for services periodically but only offer if asked for.

IV. Dispute tracking system:

A. Creditor Dispute Tracker

Creditor Dispute Tracker
Tracking disputes in 6-month intervals **or** Two Periods Per year

First period of the year:

Year:_____   Sheet #_____ OF _____   Dispute Tracking:

CRA: Initial Report

Dispute 1 CRA: Outcome	Dispute 2 CRA: Outcome	Dispute 3 CRA: Outcome	Dispute 4 CRA: Outcome	Dispute 5 CRA: Outcome	Dispute 6 CRA: Outcome
1.	1.	1.	1.	1.	1.
2.	2.	2.	2.	2.	2.
3.	3.	3.	3.	3.	3.
4.	4.	4.	4.	4.	4.
5.	5.	5.	5.	5.	5.

page ___ of ___

Creditor Dispute Tracker
Tracking disputes in 6-month intervals **or** Two Periods Per year

Second period of the year:

Year:_____   Sheet #_____ OF _____   Dispute Tracking:

CRA: Initial Report

Dispute 1 CRA: Outcome	Dispute 2 CRA: Outcome	Dispute 3 CRA: Outcome	Dispute 4 CRA: Outcome	Dispute 5 CRA: Outcome	Dispute 6 CRA: Outcome
1.	1.	1.	1.	1.	1.
2.	2.	2.	2.	2.	2.
3.	3.	3.	3.	3.	3.
4.	4.	4.	4.	4.	4.
5.	5.	5.	5.	5.	5.

page ___ of ___

B. *Individual Creditor Dispute Expenses Tracker*

Individual Creditor Dispute Expenses:

Year_____ TO _____
Creditor:_____   Page ___ OF ___

Court Costs	Postage	Proc. Service	Copies	Legal	Motions	Supplies	Phone	Travel	Misc.	TOTAL

C. Creditor expense summary tracker

Creditor expense summary:

YEAR _____ TO YEAR_____
EXPENSE SUMMARY:

SHEET #_____ OF _____

Creditor	Court Costs	Postage	Proc. Service	Copies	Legal	Motions	Supplies	Phone	Travel	Misc.	Cred.Subtotal	Running Total	Stat. Deadline

D. Dispute status tracker by bureau

DISPUTE STATUS TRACKER BY BUREAU

DISPUTE STATUS BY BUREAU:

YEAR _____ TO _____   DISPUTE T STATUS:

Creditors Disputed	EXPERIAN	EQUIFAX	TRANSUNION	OTHER
Creditors Disputed:				
Inquiries Disputed:				
Address Errors				
Telephone Errors				
Employer Errors				
Notice Errors				

Status Key:

Corrected
Removed
Pending
Incomplete

Personal Info:
AKA Errors
Creditor Complete

Page ____ OF ____

E. How to use the tracker system effectively.

The tracking system is broken into four segments. The first is a dispute tracker to track disputes filed in groups of five for each credit reporting agency and the sheet allows you to track the disputes with the credit bureau in 6-month intervals. You will need two to cover a single year's dispute tracking. If you are disputing items with more than four CRA's at a time you will need two additional sheets to cover a single year for each group of CRA's being disputed and or monitored.

The second segment is an individual expense tracker. This allows you to track expenses incurred relating to each respective creditor. You will want to insert a copy of this form in the front of each creditor folder for easy expense tracking on an ongoing basis. This will also allow you to track credits issued should this occur along the way.

The third segment is an expense summary to allow you to consolidate these expenses into a single report and allow you to keep a comprehensive total on an ongoing basis. This is composed of the totals accumulated in the individual creditor matters to allow one to determine when you break even or are made whole on losses incurred collectively.

The fourth segment is a way to allow you to track the status of individual creditor dispute outcomes by credit reporting agency. Once a creditor has been corrected on a particular bureau you insert "corrected" under the bureau on the associated creditor line. Once all bureaus containing the creditor's information are correct you then insert "completed" in the status line. If they choose to remove the items rather than correct it you then insert the word "removed" under the credit bureau on the creditor's line instead. Once the creditor has either removed or properly listed the item you then mark the status as "complete."

Again the purpose is to remove derogatory items from the report to enable one's score to rise. The dispute status tracker is grouped in sub categories that correspond to that of the credit reporting agencies. The CRA's break the report into the following categories: creditor, individual trade line entries, inquiries or those that have accessed the report in the last 24 months, and personal information. The personal information section is broken into the following sub categories: AKA or also known as, prior addresses, prior telephone numbers, current and prior employer listings and notices. The notices section are addresses that have been used for the purpose of legal service and may be different from those listed in the address section. This section is common if the person is self-employed or listed as the officer of a corporation. The address is the address shown on file for the officer for the purpose of legal notice.

F. Certified Mail Confirmation Tracker

Sample Of Package Receipt

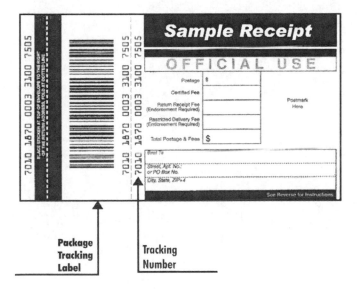

You will note along the edge a series of numbers. This is the tracking number for the certified mailing. This allows you to go to www.usps.com and click on tracking and enter the number from the slip.

Below you will see a screen shot to allow you to see an example

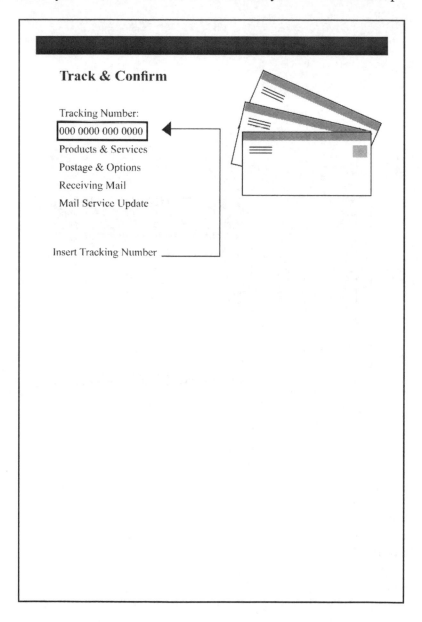

When the search is performed you will see a tracking path that the package has taken and will allow you to know exactly when

received. This receipt of the package begins the 30-day clock allowed per the FCRA for investigation of disputed item to be performed.

Package Tracking

Sign In
FAQs

Sample
Package Tracking

Search

Enter Label/ Receipt Number

Track & Confirm
Search Results:
Enter Label/ Receipt Number: xxx xxx xxxx xxx xxxx
Status: Delivered

Your Item xxx xxx xxxx xxx xxxx, was deivered at 11:04 am on Februrary 17, 2010, in SAGINAW, MI 48602. A record of proof may be available through you local Post Office for a fee

IV. Letter Samples Grouped Categorically for Easy Reference

Disclaimer:
These letters are not to be deemed legal advice but rather merely sample letters that I have used in my identity recapture process. The letters derive from letters done by attorneys in my behalf that I simply modified for future use in other matters. Use them as you deem appropriate and not held liable for said letter sample's use.

Letter to Acquire copy of CRA Report (for industry reports):
Sample #1:

Month ___, ____

CRA by name (see chapter 12 for CRA contacts)
Address
City, State, Zip code

To Whom It May Concern:
I am entitled to a free copy of my report file with __
(CRA)_____(www._____.com) maintained under my Social
Security number. Thus I am formally requesting a complete
copy of my report in accordance with my FCRA rights at no
cost to me. This request is to include all reports including but
not limited to auto insurance, home insurance, personal claims
and any other similar reports on file with ___(CRA)____
under said Social Security number with __(CRA)____or its
affiliates, subsidiaries, successors and or assigns. In the event
no records are found please provide written confirmation
to this effect in accordance with the FCRA within the
required statutory period required not exceeding 30 days.

I do not have derogatory items. If I learn to the
contrary you will be facing legal action.

Please validate and provide me with copies of any
documentation associated with this "said accounts". In the
absence of any such documentation bearing my signature I
ask that this information be immediately deleted from the file
you maintain under my Social Security number. I will expect
information to be complete; any partial files are to be deleted
or face additional legal action for listed inaccurate information
under the Fair Credit Reporting Act, Fair Debt Collections
Practices Act, other federal laws and statutes. You have 30
days as required by law to provide requested information.
My contact information is as follows:

First Name, Middle Initial, Last Name (how you sign your name)
SSN: XXX-XX-XXXX
ADDRESS: ### Street, City, State, Zip code

Sincerely,

(insert name as you sign it)

NOTE: (recommend first name, middle initial, last name) (this will help alleviate AKA's or aliases)
(attach proof of identity, send by certified mail)

NOTE #2: (MODIFY LETTER TO REFLECT THE CRA YOU ARE CONTACTING SO IF INDUSTIES LISTED DO NOT APPLY REMOVE THEM. THE LETTER SAMPLE IS MEANT TO SERVE AS A FOUNDATIONAL STRUCTURE FOR YOUR LETTER.).

Note #3: ALL LETTERS SHOULD BE DONE IN SIZE 12 FONT (standard font style)

Letter to Acquire copy of CRA Report (for Traditional CRA'S):

Sample #2:

Month ___, ____

CRA by name (see chapter 12 for CRA contacts)
Address
City, State, Zip code

To Whom It May Concern:
I am entitled to a free copy of my report file with __
(CRA)_____(www._____.com(if they have a web site)
maintained under my Social Security number. Thus I
am formally requesting a complete copy of my report in
accordance with my FCRA rights at no cost to me. This
request is to include all reports including all reports on
file with ___(CRA)_____under said Social Security
number with ___(CRA)_____or its affiliates, subsidiaries,
successors and or assigns. In the event no records are
found please provide written confirmation to this effect
in accordance with the FCRA within the required
statutory period required not exceeding 30 days.

I do not have derogatory items. If I learn to the
contrary you will be facing legal action.

Please validate and provide me with copies of any
documentation associated with this "said accounts". In the
absence of any such documentation bearing my signature I
ask that this information be immediately deleted from the file
you maintain under my Social Security number. I will expect
information to be complete any partial files are to be deleted
or face additional legal action for listed inaccurate information
under the Fair Credit Reporting Act, Fair Debt Collections
Practices Act, other federal laws and statutes. You have 30
days as required by law to provide requested information.
My contact information is as follows:

First Name, Middle Initial, Last Name (how you sign your name)
SSN: XXX-XX-XXXX
ADDRESS: ### Street, City, State, Zip code

Sincerely,

(insert name as you sign it)

NOTE:(recommend first name, middle initial, last name) (this will help alleviate AKA's or aliases)
(attach proof of identity, send by certified mail)

Letter to Dispute 5 items in a CRA Report:

Sample #3:

(First Name, Middle Initial, Last Name)
Address
City, State, Zip code

CRA
CRA Address
CRA City, State, Zip code (reference
chapter 12 for contact information)

Month ___, _____(month, day, year)

Attention: Consumer Dispute Investigation:

I am requesting Verification of Negative Items shown on
my credit report. As you know, the Fair Credit Reporting
Act requires you Follow Reasonable Procedures to Assume
Maximum Possible Accuracy of the information on my
Report. Accordingly, I am Requesting you Verify the items
I am Disputing at a Higher Standard than a Computer
Generated Inquiry or Third Party Database Search. Also,
please Notify each Source that reported these items within
(5) days after Receiving this Dispute and obtain either

**VERBAL OR WRITTEN PROOF DIRECTLY FROM
A PERSON AT THAT SOURCE PURSUANT TO: 15
USC Section 611 (i)(7) & Section (6) (I)(iii) of the FCRA.**

Verify with the person, my Full Name, Address, Date of Birth,
Social Security, Status & Date of last Activity and Balance
Amount (if applicable). If any one article of these points of
information listed is inaccurate or incomplete, the entire entry
must be deleted. When you have finished your investigation, I
want the Name, Address & Telephone Number of the person

at each Source you contacted as the law requires you to do
and also a corrected Updated Copy of my credit report.

I will Expect you to Complete your investigation
Within 30 Calendar days from the Date you receive
this Dispute with All the Information Detailed in
the foregoing paragraph as Mandated in the FCRA
Statutes or the items being Disputed will be

UNVERIFIABLE & SUBJECT TO DELETION.
The items appear on my credit report as follows:
#1. Sample name correction (Name identification number
(___(from report)_____)
#2. Second sample name error (Name identification number
_____)
#3. Insert Creditor name partial ACT#
(insert number from report)

#4. Sample entry (collection) enter collector name
partial ACT# (insert number from report)

#5. Sample False agency (insert name) partial
ACT# (insert number from report)

These inaccuracies are extremely detrimental to my credit
profile and the reason for each item disputed is as follows:

#1. (insert reason)
#2. (insert reason)
#3. (insert reason)
#4. (insert reason)
#5. (insert reason)

Very truly yours,

First name, Middle Initial, Last Name)

NOTE: (recommend first name, middle initial, last name) (this
will help alleviate AKA's or aliases)
(attach proof of identity, send by certified mail)

NOTE #2: (I inserted samples in the letter above to give you
a spectrum of possible dispute types you might encounter)

NOTE #3: (Be sure to include creditor name,
partial account # or identification number and the
reason for dispute on each respective matter)

Letter of dispute due to failure to comply with prior request due to statutory time line:
Sample #4:

(First Name, Middle Initial, Last Name)
Address
City, State, Zip code
Sample #4:

CRA
CRA Address
CRA City, State, Zip code (reference
chapter 12 for contact information)

Month ___, _____(month, day, year)

Attention: Consumer Dispute investigations:

I'm writing this letter at the direction and advice of my
attorney. On (DATE)_____, I mailed you a request for
the "method of verification" used to verify derogatory
information shown on my credit report. According to www.
usps.com you received my request on __(DATE)___. I have
attached a copy of the delivery confirmation showing the date
you received my dispute as well as a copy of the request.

You have failed to provide a detailed description
of the methods used to verify the information
disputed as the law requires you to do.

Furthermore, you also failed to provide me with the
name of the person at the sources you contacted, the
furnisher's business name, address and phone number/
OR the furnisher's contact information you provided
has verified they are not the actual furnisher.

**YOU ARE IN DIRECT VIOLATION OF THE FAIR
CREDIT REPORTING ACT.
ACCORDINGLY, THE ITEMS UNDER
DISPUTE MUST BE DELETED.**

**I WILL EXPECT THIS MATTER TO BE RESOLVED
WITHIN 30 DAYS AND AN UPDATED CREDIT REPORT
SENT TO ME WITH THE DISPUTED ITEMS DELETED.**

You are hereby advised if it is not and you continue to
willfully violate the FCRA, my attorney has informed me,
he will follow through in my behalf. He will be contacting
my state Congressional Representative for procedural
action through the Attorney General and FTC, as I stated
in my previous letter, without further notice to you.

Very truly yours,

(First Name, Middle Initial, Last Name)

NOTE: (recommend First Name, Middle Initial, Last Name)
(this will help alleviate AKA's or aliases)
(attach proof of identity, send by certified mail)

Letter of dispute due to claim of verified as accurate:
Sample #5:

(First Name, Middle Initial, Last Name)
Address
City, State, Zip code

CRA
CRA Address
CRA City, State, Zip code (reference
chapter 12 for contact information)

Month ___, _____(month, day, year)

CRA Report # :

Attention: Consumer Dispute investigations:

on_____ __,____ , I mailed you a request for the verification
of negative items being reported to my credit report. Thank
you for completing your investigation within 30 days. As you
know, the Fair Credit Reporting Act requires you to follow
specific rules and procedures when verifying information.

You have failed to provide me with a detailed description of
the method of verification used by your agency and the name
of the person at each source you contacted, the furnisher's
business name, address, and phone number as mandated by
the Fair Credit Reporting Act **15 USC SECTION 611(I)(7) and
SECTION (6)(i)(III) as requested by me in my initial letter.**

YOU HAVE 15 CALENDAR DAYS TO
COMPLETE THIS REQUEST.

If you cannot provide a detailed description of the method of verification and the contact information of the furnisher, you are in violation of procedure and must delete the items.

If you ignore this request or provide insufficient or incomplete response, I will have no other alternative choice but to contact my state Congressional Representative who will forward this matter promptly to the Attorney General and Federal Trade Commission for urgent attention and appropriate action.

Thank you.

Very Truly Yours,

(First Name, Middle Initial, Last Name)

NOTE: (recommend First Name, Middle Initial, Last Name) (this will help alleviate AKA's or aliases)

(attach proof of identity, send by certified mail)

Letter sent when the 30 day period has expired without compliance:
Sample #6:

(First Name, Middle Initial, Last Name)
Address
City, State, Zip code

CRA
CRA Address
CRA City, State, Zip code (reference
chapter 12 for contact information)

Month ___, _____(month, day, year)

Attention: Consumer Dispute investigations:

On____ __, ____(date), I mailed you a request for
the verification of derogatory information shown
on my credit report. According to www.usps.com
you received my dispute on _____ __.____(date).
I have attached a copy of the delivery confirmation
showing the date you received my dispute.

**However, you did not complete your investigation
within 30 days pursuant to the section 611(a)
(I) of the Fair Credit Reporting Act.**

**THEREFORE, THE ITEMS UNDER
DISPUTE MUST BE DELETED.**

I will expect this matter to be resolved within 30 days.

If you ignore this request or provide an insufficient or incomplete response I will have no other choice but to contact my Congressional Representative who will promptly forward this matter to the Attorney General and the Federal Trade Commission for urgent attention and action.

Thank you.

Sincerely,

(First Name, Middle Initial, Last Name)

NOTE:(recommend First Name, Middle Initial, Last Name) (this will help alleviate AKA's or aliases)

(attach proof of identity, send by certified mail)

Letter to be used if prior removed item is reinserted without provocation:
Sample #7:

Attention: Consumer Dispute investigations:

I mailed you a dispute letter on _____ __, ____(date) and
the results of your investigation ended in the deletion
of the items listed below. However, the items below
have been reinserted without you properly notifying
me as required by the Fair Credit Reporting Act.

As you know, under Section 611 you are required to notify
me not later than 5 business days after the date of the
reinsertion by any means available. **YOU FAILED TO
NOTIFY ME** and are now in violation of federal law.

Therefore, I am requesting you delete the items and
permanently block them from being reinserted in the future.

The items that were reinserted were as follows:

#1.

#2.

#3.

#4.

#5.

I will expect the matter to be resolved within 30 days.

If you ignore this request I will have no other choice but
to contact my state Congressional Representative who
will promptly forward this matter to the appropriate

authorities. This shall include but not be limited to the Attorney General, Federal Trade Commission and other similar governmental bodies for urgent attention.

Thank you.

Very Truly Yours,

(First name, Middle initials, Last Name)

NOTE: (recommend First Name, Middle Initial, Last Name) (this will help alleviate AKA's or aliases)

(attach proof of identity, send by certified mail)

NOTE #1: (Be sure to include creditor name, partial account # or identification number and the reason for dispute on each respective matter)

Letter to be used if congressional office is required to be contacted to resolve:
Sample #8:

(First Name, Middle Initial, Last Name)
Address
City, State, Zip code

CRA
CRA Address
CRA City, State, Zip code (reference
chapter 12 for contact information)

Month ___, _____(month, day, year)

Dear Congressman & or office staff person;

Pursuant to our conversation on ____ __,____(date), please
forward the enclosed documents (copies of prior disputes with
proof received) to ___ (insert CRA name).They are as follows:

( ) Ignoring my dispute with total disregard to procedures
mandated by the Fair Credit Reporting Act.

( ) In direct violation of___ **day time limit procedure**
imposed under the Fair Credit Reporting Act.

( ) Not providing me any contact information regarding
the furnisher or source of the alleged derogatory items
as required by the Fair Credit Reporting Act.

( ) Not providing me accurate contact information
regarding the furnisher or source of the alleged derogatory
items as required by the Fair Credit Reporting Act.

The attached documentation will show the information
I have rightfully asked for is not being provided
by___(CRA NAME). It is imperative they now
delete the items disputed as mandated by law.

In addition, I am requesting(CRA NAME) provide me written
confirmation this matter has been permanently resolved, and
a corrected copy of my credit report. Thank you for your
assistance in forwarding this matter to the parties listed below:

Very truly yours,

(First Name, Middle Initial, Last Name)

PLEASE FORWARD TO: CRA & ADDRESS

**PLEASE FORWARD TO: STATE
ATTORNEY GENERAL & ADDRESS**

PLEASE FORWARD TO:

> **Federal Trade Commission**
> Consumer Response Center
> 600 Pennsylvania Avenue, NW
> Washington, DC 20580

NOTE: (recommend First Name, Middle Initial, Last
Name) (this will help alleviate AKA's or aliases)

(attach proof of identity, send by certified mail)

NOTE #2:(Be sure to include prior disputes & proof received)

Letter to be used as final attempt to resolve before federal suit is filed:
Sample #9:

(First Name, Middle Initial, Last Name)
Address
City, State, Zip code

FINAL NOTICE BEFORE SUIT

CRA
CRA Address
CRA City, State, Zip code (reference
chapter 12 for contact information)

Month ___, _____(month, day, year)

Attention Legal Department:

To whom it may concern:

You are hereby advised, if the disputed items listed below of
this final communication are not removed from my credit
report, legal proceedings will be initiated against you in
Federal District Court _____ County, _____County
,____City,__State,_____ Zip Code for continual and willful
violation of the Fair Credit Reporting Act statutes.

You have 30 calendar days from the receipt of this final notice to remove the disputed items from my credit report and provide me an updated copy with the disputed items deleted.

#1. (insert creditor name, partial account number or identification #)

#2.

#3.

#4.

#5.

No further notification will be given you.

Very truly yours,

(First Name, Middle Initial, Last Name)

NOTE: (recommend First Name, Middle Initial, Last Name) (this will help alleviate AKA's or aliases)

(attach proof of identity, send by certified mail)

Letter to remove unauthorized inquires listed on a cra:

Sample #10:

(First Name, Middle Initial, Last Name)

Address

City, State, Zip code

CRA
CRA Address
CRA City, State, Zip code (reference
chapter 12 for contact information)

Month ___, _____(month, day, year)

Attention Legal Department:

Your company placed an unauthorized inquiry
on my credit report on ____ __,____.

Either provide me conclusive proof I authorized you
to inquire, such as a signed contract or recorded
telephone call or DELETE the items immediately.

Under 15 USC Section 623 you have 30 days to
do a reasonable inquiry into this matter.

Please be advised, if you ignore this letter and do not
delete the inquiry or don't provide documented proof of
the -authorization, I will have no other choice but to file an
action against _____(name firm),____(company),____(CRA

by name),_____pursuant to Section 616 & 617 of the Fair
Credit Reporting Act or have my local congressman promptly
forward a formal complaint to the Federal Trade Commission
and Attorney General for further scrutiny of this matter.

Thank you.

Sincerely,

(First Name, Middle Initial, Last Name)

NOTE: (recommend First Name, Middle Initial, Last
Name) (this will help alleviate AKA's or aliases)

(attach proof of identity, send by certified mail)

Letter to be used to stop collection agency harrasment by phone & mail:
Sample #11:

(First Name, Middle Initial, Last Name)

Address

City, State, Zip code

_____ __,____(DATE)

ATTENTION:

NAME OF COLLECTION FIRM

Address

City, State, Zip code

Account#:_____

Name of Creditor:_____

NOTICE TO CEASE & DESIST

As of the date indicated above, pursuant to Federal law, To Wit, the Fair Debt Collections Practices Act, Title # 15 U.S.C.S. Section 1692C, paragraph C, YOU ARE

**HEREBY ORDERED TO IMMEDIATELY CEASE
AND DESIST FROM ANY FURTHER CONTACT
(DIRECTLY OR INDIRECTLY) WITH ME. (Exception
of One Final Communication Permitted Under the Act)**

**If you ignore this notice, charges will be initiated against
you for willful Non Compliance of Federal Statutes.**

(First Name, Middle Initial, Last Name)

NOTE: (recommend First Name, Middle Initial, Last
Name) (this will help alleviate AKA's or aliases)

(attach proof of identity, send by certified mail)

Letter to be used to put creditor on notice that continued violations will not be tolerated:
Sample #12:

(First Name, Middle Initial, Last Name)

Address

City, State, Zip code

CRA or Creditor
CRA Address
CRA City, State, Zip code (reference
chapter 12 for contact information)

Month ____, _____(month, day, year)

Acct#:_____-

To whom it may concern,

Please be advised that I will, if necessary, retain
counsel to prosecute a federal court action arising
from the failure of _____(creditor)___ to comply
with the requirements of 15USC1681 et seq.

It is my intention to seek from you and your company not only
compensatory but also punitive damages and attorney fees, as
statutorily provided. I have suffered substantially monetary
loss as well as emotional distress and professional libel as a
result of your ongoing reporting of inaccurate and misleading
credit information regarding the account noted above. I intend
to hold you responsible and I am legally entitled to do so.

The purpose of this letter is a final attempt to provide (___(CREDITOR)_____ and yourself with a last opportunity to rectify your error and thereby avoid what will surely be lengthy and costly litigation.

You have reported to (Specify CRA's) that the above identified account was delinquent and status as____(INSERT STATUS)_____, when was (specify sold, inaccurate, invalidated, etc. and only on relevant characteristics). Not only is that reporting incorrect, it is misleading as well.

This inaccuracy has been brought to your attention on multiple occasions including communications from the (Honorable Congressman _____office (or reference prior dispute) in which you clearly stated this very point of error, yet you have declined to correct it. This has caused me both professional and personal damage of both an economic and non-economic nature.

The fact of the matter is that I, Mr. (__ NAME)____ have disputed the item's accuracy and the 30 day statutory period has now expired and the item is now required to be deleted without exception. Therefore no payments were due as a result of the sale. If no payments were due, none could logically be delinquent. This is besides the status designation error noted above and both are cause for action on my part against you.

As I am sure you are aware, the FCRA requires not only that information reported to a CRA by a furnisher such as yourself be accurate, that information must also not be misleading (see Dalton v. Capitol Assoc. 257F.3d409). The information reported by you is both inaccurate and misleading. You have been made aware of this error and under the relevant portions of the FCRA you are obligated to correct this error by now deleting the account in its entirety without exception.

Failure to do so amounts to malice and/or willful wanton misconduct on your part (see sec1681,2,(a),(1),(A)) which would take your actions outside of the protection of the limited immunity conferred by 15 USC 1681h and subjects you to liability for numerous tort causes of action including but not limited to intentional infliction of emotional distress, injurious falsehood, and intentional interference with prospective contractual relationships.

This is in addition to several pendant state statutory claims that fall outside of the Federal preemption statutes.

In short, I have been defamed. The only course of action would now be to simply delete the account information in its entirety as required per the statute. Failure to do so will be costly. If you fail to comply I will turn the matter over to my attorney ___(INSERT NAME)_____for prosecution in Federal Court ____(INSERT CITY)___, ___(INSERT COUNTY)_____.

Sincerely,

(First Name, Middle Initial, Last Name)

cc: Appropriately applicable CRA's (Transunion, Experian, Equifax, etc. as relevant)

cc:

cc:

enclosures: included

NOTE: (recommend First Name, Middle Initial, Last Name) (this will help alleviate AKA's or aliases)

(attach proof of identity, send by certified mail)

Letter to add positive accounts to bureaus that they do not currently report to:

Sample #13:

(First Name, Middle Initial, Last Name)
Address
City, State, Zip code

Month ___, _____(month, day, year)

CRA OR Creditor
CRA Address
CRA City, State, Zip code (reference chapter
12 for contact information)

ATTN: Consumer Relations Department

To whom it may concern:

At your earliest opportunity, please include the
following credit references to my credit report:

	Business Name	**Business Telephone#**	**Account #**
#1.	_____	_____	_____
#2.	_____	_____	_____
#3.	_____	_____	_____
#4.	_____	_____	_____
#5.	_____	_____	_____

Please send an updated report to me after the above has been completed. If there is any expense for the service, please advise me.

Thank you for your expeditious cooperation.

Very truly yours,

(First Name, Middle initial, Last Name)

cc: Trans union consumer relations (if applicable)

cc: Equifax (if applicable)

cc: Experian (if applicable)

enclosures: included

NOTE: (recommend First Name, Middle Initial, Last Name) (this will help alleviate AKA's or aliases)

(attach proof of identity, send by certified mail)

V. *Sample reasons of creditor or credit bureau complaint:*

(THIS IS MEANT TO SERVE AS A STARTER LIST
THAT YOU CAN REFINE TO YOUR SITUATION)

This is not my account.

Due to (insert highly specific reason) I am not
responsible for payment delivery delay.

This entry is the result of identity theft or credit fraud.

Contact this creditor for an explanation of this item's content.

The date of last activity of this listing is beyond 7 years and
thus obsolete and required to be removed without exception.

This was a billing error and should not
appear for any reason within report.

The creditor billed the wrong address (and
is aware of their error if applicable).

The payment was never late and the original
creditor has failed to prove so.

The creditor has incorrectly listed me as in default
after assigning the loan to another party.

The account was paid off and never late.

The (insert erroneous specific item) of
the listing is not accurate.

The account is incorrect due to creditor error.

The (insert account) bankruptcy court
will verify the item is incorrect.

The item is not included in bankruptcy.

This listing is obsolete and required to be removed
without exception due to account age.

The automobile was returned under the state's
Lemon Law and is not a repossession.

The car loan was paid on time and has
been listed as repossession in error.

The creditor has incorrectly listed me as in default
after assigning the account to another party.

The inquiry was not authorized and is required
to be removed without exception.

Budget sample worksheet:

MERRITT & ASSOCIATES INC." Planning with Merit"

Name_____

Six Month Cash Flow Summary   Date_____

Please go back six months in your checkbook or receipts and fill in the exact amounts.

	Month 1	Month 2	Month 3	Month 4	Month 5	Month 6	Once a year
Expenses							
House/Rent							
Electricity							
Natural Gas/Propane							
Telephone							
Water/Sewer/Trash							
Taxes							
Car Payments							
Gas							
Car Insurance							
Car Maintenance							
Food							
Clothing							
Medical/Dental							
Drugs/Medicine							
Laundry/Cleaning							
Gifts							
Contributions							
Haircuts							
House Maintenance							
Medical Insurance							
Disability Insurance							
Life Insurance							
Savings							
Vacation Savings							

	Month 1	Month 2	Month 3	Month 4	Month 5	Month 6	Once a year
Investment Savings							
Credit Card-Total Owed							
1. $							
2. $							
3. $							
4. $							
5 $							
6. $							
7. $							
Adult Continuing Ed.							
Primary Ed.							
Secondary Ed.							
College Ed.							
Newspaper/Periodicals							
Entertainment							
Babysitting							
Cash							
TOTAL OUTLAY							
Net Paycheck							
Net Paycheck							
Net Investment Income							
TOTAL NET INCOME							
BALANCE + or -							

Good Foundation

Legal Foundation

Personal Asset Ownership Control

Business Asset Ownership Control

Financial Power Of Attorney

Living Will

Asset titling

Medical Power Of Attorney

Trust

Corporation

Financial FoundationCore Of Success

Personal Credit Worthiness As an Asset

Establishment Of Business Credit Worthiness

Establishment Of Personal Credit Worthiness

Business Credit Worthiness As an Asset

Ground Foundation From Which All Future Financial Success Is Built

House Of Financial Sucess

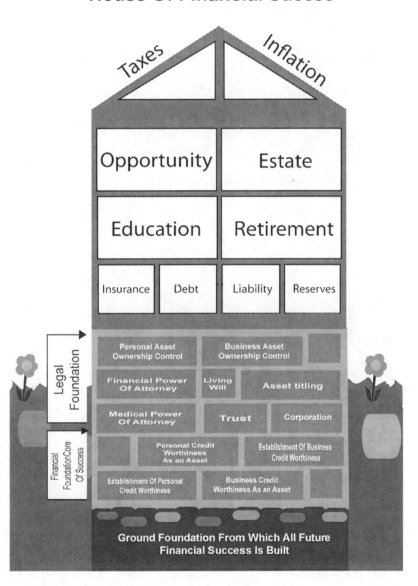

For reader related resources and additional books to follow
in the Building Your Financial House of Success Series
SEE www.planningwithmerit.com

CPSIA information can be obtained at www.ICGtesting.com
Printed in the USA
LVOW11s1531040414

380379LV00011B/615/P